THE QUESTIONS YOU ASKED

QUESTIONS ON JEWISH BELIEF AND THE ANSWERS OF A LIBERAL RABBI

Morrison David Bial

Rabbi, Temple Sinai of Summit

BEHRMAN HOUSE, INC.

My gratitude to Constance Reiter and the teachers of the Temple Sinai Religious School, who tried out much of this material; and to Marygray Cherry and Andrew Ansel for their help, and especially to my wife, Dorothy Diona, for her discernment.

I am grateful to Daisy and Isidor M. Gross for funding the experimental material leading to this edition.

Most of all I thank the officers, trustees and members of Temple Sinai of Summit for their inspiration and cooperation. It is to them that I dedicate this book as together we observe the twentieth anniversary of the founding of the congregation — and approach my own twentieth anniversary with them as well.

To the Reader

There are many questions on the Jewish conceptions of God, religion and ethics that come to the mind of any thinking person. They are questions of belief, of the origin of belief, or of the relationship of ethics to religion and to life.

No book on theology can answer them all—and neither can this one. They demand the give and take of discussion and some knowledge of the Torah, the rabbis of the Talmud and the Midrash, and of our later sages.

This book attempts to provide the basis for such a dialogue. The questions are those most often asked. The answers are those of a Liberal rabbi, and are meant for either Reform or Conservative Jews—or for non-Jews interested in modern Judaism. The author does not expect to answer any question to every person's satisfaction. He does hope that he is able to indicate the general response of Judaism to these questions.

If I am able to provide sufficient information so that you are stimulated to read, to contemplate and to find a position that is positive and satisfying to you, then I will have fulfilled the purpose of this work. You may or may not like my answers, or even my mode of thought, but if they serve as a catalyst to your own thinking, then for you my work will have attained its goal.

Morrison David Bial

"Whosoever serves God out of love, occupies himself with the study of the Torah and the fulfillment of commandments and walks in the paths of wisdom, impelled by no external motive, moved neither by fear of calamity nor the desire to obtain material benefits—such a person does what is truly right because it is truly right . . . . "

Maimonides, Mishneh Torah, Knowledge 10:2

To the Instructor

The questions we are to consider came from a variety of sources. The major source is a survey conducted by the Commission on Education (CCAR–UAHC) under the supervision of Rabbi Jack Spiro to determine the questions, issues and problems that concern young Jews. Questions from other sources are included. The questions were winnowed to seek those that seemed most interesting and pertinent and would lead to discussions. Few of the questions included here require factual answers. What is vital is that most of them admit no easy response, no answers which can be looked up in a reference work.

The teacher or leader who presents these questions will be touching areas which are of concern to most people. Enabling them to discuss and find meaningful answers should be of immediate importance. Any thoughtful person, young or adult, must find some position of awareness dealing with these matters as they are the basic stuff of individual philosophy and faith— and the essence of Judaism.

The Purpose of the Book

The purpose of this book is to provoke discussion as a means to learning, leading to a positively oriented Judaism. The writer is a Liberal rabbi. He has tried to respond so that the broad stream of both Reform and Conservative Jewry will find this work congenial. Nor does it attack the most traditional positions of Orthodox Judaism, though it will disagree in some measure.

The material is meant to be a solid part of a year's work, or even better, to be used regularly over a longer period. Projects, further reading, consultations with the rabbi or other resource people may extend our voyage of discovery.

Whatever you do, please do not just read the question and answer to your group and feel that duty has been done. Each question demands individual and careful consideration. You might submit the question the week before.

You may require a brief written response or that each be discussed at home or contemplated at leisure.

Do not be afraid of disagreement with the answers here presented—or with any traditional answer. Judaism has no official creed. Individuals have always been allowed to arrive at their own philosophies, within very broad boundaries. Only if the group response is negative must you take issue. Any divergence in answer that is positive is welcome. Of course you present your own thinking, but try not to impose it on the group. It should merely be one more strand in the web.

Nota bene

The answers provided here are not necessarily those you will find satisfying, nor do they attempt to be complete. The material is meant to supply direction to you and your group. The answers should be a starting point for discussion. Or they may be used as resource when group response is sparse. At times the question alone plus a brief introduction will suffice, as the participants will supply their own contributions, which may be more satisfying to them than what is offered here.

This book contains the thinking of one rabbi. Other rabbis may disagree, as will some lay people. Agree with my answers or disagree with them, but try to arouse your group to consider seriously how their own reactions may affect for the better their life philosophies—and as such be of the utmost importance. If you can arouse your group to spirited and considered discussion, some of them may learn to be better human beings and Jews—and that is your prime role as teacher or leader.

Contents

THE JEWISH PEOPLE

LIFE AND DEATH

JUDAISM AND CHRISTIANITY

Why is the Sh'ma considered the unique expression of the Jewish faith?

There are historical and emotional reasons why the *Sh'ma* has been central in our worship and our belief. It has been the expression of the oneness and the unity of God for centuries. It is recited twice every day by our traditional brothers. It was the sentence on the lips of Jewish martyrs as they died for *Kiddush HaShem*, the Sanctification of God's name.

There are other reasons which are equally pertinent. Reaffirming God's unity is a bond with the past and is also a bond with every fellow Jew. The recital of the *Sh'ma* has been called the Jewish creed, as the one line separates us from worshipers of dual or triune gods, from pagans, and from worshipers of Allah — and yet by insisting on God's oneness as well as His uniqueness, it reaffirms our belief that all men are God's children, and hence our brothers. While the *Sh'ma* indicates our belonging to one people and one religion, it also avers that we are one with God and all humanity. The *Sh'ma* distinguishes; it does not separate.

God is the Prime Loyalty

The *Sh'ma* states that there is only one God, who alone in the cosmos is eternal, absolute and infinite. Only He may be worshiped. To Him is our prime loyalty, not to any country, or philosophy, or society. What is more, our loyalties to any country, philosophy or society must be in consonance with that for which God stands.

The *Sh'ma* describes God as unity and being. The value of life stems from comprehension of His values, His standards, ethical and spiritual. Faith in God is not only worship and trust, though they are part of faith. Faith is also loyalty to God and service in His creative cause.

If we comprehend this, we then must recognize that man can live only relative to God. All standards, all criteria to have validity must be established in relationship to God's verities, His existence, that for which He stands.

Even with all our study of the Torah and the world's philosophies, we realize that our best thinking is at best only partial. We can never truly comprehend God. But the recital of the *Sh'ma* should be a constant reminder to us so that we may use the thrust of our loyalty to Him, the best thinking of our minds, to establish a climate of faith and dedication to provoke us to live and to work actively in God's service.

What is God?

The rabbis never tried to answer this question, "What is God?" To them God was, He is, He will be. He is beyond time. He is also beyond any of our descriptions or attempts at interpretation. Any term we would use is man-made, the product of our finite minds, and even the most discerning words cannot begin to be fitting.

The rabbis sometimes said that we cannot say what God is, but we can describe what He does. The prophet Jeremiah spoke in God's name of those who would attempt to understand Him: "Let him who wishes to glory glory in this, that he understands and knows Me, that I am the Lord who practices kindness, justice and righteousness in the earth, for in these things do I delight" (9:23).

God identified Himself to the Israelites at Sinai, "I am the Lord your God, who brought you out of the land of Egypt, out of the house of bondage" (Exodus 20:2). Names do not identify Him. Only His deeds do, only the response He wins in men's hearts. This is why the Bible always presents God as a most personal God. He is not only the Creator of the world, He is the *Ribono shel Olam*, the Master of the Universe, who is concerned with all. In the words of the late Henry Slonimsky, "When I pray to God, I think of an old Jew with a skullcap and a beard, who sits just above me and responds, 'I know, my son!'

The great Hasidic sage, Schneour Zalman of Ladi, answered this question, "All I know is God. He is clearly present in everything I know, and without Him nothing is clearly present."

God is the great illuminator of life as well as the great teacher of moral purpose. God is spirit within all. When this spirit reaches out toward the spirit in others, then spirit touching spirit enkindles life and illumines the meaning and purpose of God.

What is love of God?

Love of God must not be adulation. A love such as that of Petrarch for Laura, in which he stood at a distance and adored her, never daring to address her, is not love but adulation. It is far beneath the level of love. In real love there is give and take, there is working together to form a bond that can weather time and tribulation.

Love of God must be an active, on-going love. The prophets spoke of the relationship between God and Israel in terms of the love of a bridegroom for his bride, and her reciprocating in devotion. The Midrash and the medieval commentators understood the Song of Songs as depicting a spiritual marriage between God and Israel. As love between God and man can transfigure and hallow, so the love between God and man can become a *shalhevet Yah*, a "flame of the Lord."

Love is expressed in dedication, in trust. Love of God must be straightforward, to live by His ways, fulfilling His expectations of our life. We cannot possess God; we can be possessed by Him. Such possession does not blind us to our fellow men, but rather should awaken our recognition of the godhead within them.

A Love That Ennobles

Love of God must enkindle and ennoble. He who says he loves God and commits any crime against the least of His creatures is unfaithful and desecrates the very idea of love. We can never love God sufficiently, yet the act of loving must bring us to recognize how we must try to be worthy of His love for us.

It is written, "Praise the Lord, O my soul" (Psalms 103:1). As the soul fills the body, so does God fill the world. As the soul keeps the body alive, so does God keep the world alive. As the soul outlives the body, so does God outlive the world. As there is only one soul in one body, so there is one God in all the world. As the soul is pure in the body, so God is pure in the world. So let the soul which is pure in the body praise God who is pure in the world (Lev. Rabba Vayikra 4:8; Berachot 10a).

Is God real?

God is real. You are real. You did not exist a number of years ago. You will not exist 100 years from now. You maintain you are real. God has been here a lot longer than you and will be long after you are gone. Friedrich Nietzsche, the German iconoclast, wrote a proclamation, "God is dead!" and signed it. A few years later a wag put up another proclamation, "Nietzsche is dead!" and signed it "God."

This is a joke and it is not a joke for there is truth in it. Man and God are not real in the same sense. We cannot use terms which describe man to describe God. God's existence is not temporal or physical. We speak of God's reality in very different terms. He is the spirit which undergirds all existence. Underlying the whole cosmos is God. There is order in the cosmos, in all the physical world. There are teachings of spirit and ethic which we recognize are basic to all human life. There is creativity, love and beauty. They cannot be the product of chance.

Beyond this is the world of spirit. There are tens of millions of religious people who firmly believe that they have real contact with God. He has touched their lives or spoken to them or responded in some significant way. Some of these manifestations may be the product of emotion or superstition or wishful thinking. Only a cynic would attempt to deny validity to all of this.

The Bible as God's Word

There is the Bible with its solid mass of evidence of God's spirit moving in man. To maintain that all of the spiritual and ethical genius of the Bible just happened is to accept something far harder to understand than that there is true spirit which inspired hundreds of men and women over a period of a thousand years.

Hundreds of millions of thinking human beings have found strength and response in prayer and rite. Are they all victims of delusion? They include most of the greatest minds we have had upon earth. Any selection of the greatest minds in human history would be replete with religious contributors to the betterment of the world. Were Moses and Buddha, Isaiah and Zoroaster, Hillel and Jesus, Maimonides and Muhammed all charlatans or deluded — while you or someone in your group is so much wiser than they?

You Stand Before Your Own Mind

But you react, you are an individual with your own mind and your own responsibilities to think, to evaluate, to decide for yourself. You may be guided by the teachings and examples of Moses or David or Amos, but Judaism itself says you must make up your own mind.

True, entirely true. Judaism says you are responsible to live out your own answer to this question, "Is God real in your life?" By answering "yes" you accept a challenge that is noble, to make your life meaningful before God and man. This is the only positive answer to this question.

What do the names of God mean?

According to Jewish lore there are seventy names of God. Some are supposedly secret and known only to the initiate in mysticism, and a few are unknown even to them. But there are many which are known to anyone who reads Hebrew.

The most important is the name which we do not know how to pronounce, represented by the four Hebrew letters *yod hei vav hei*. It is reproduced in English as YHVH or Yahveh (sometimes Jahweh or Yahweh). The correct vowels are not known to any person. The name was pronounced only on Yom Kippur by the High Priest, in the Temple on Mount Moriah. He transmitted the pronunciation to his two eldest sons, but it has been lost since the destruction of the Temple in the year 70 C.E.

The name is probably derived from the Hebrew verb "to be." It is a variant of God's answer to Moses when he asks His name, *eheyeh asher eheyeh* (Ex. 3:14), which can be translated as "I am what I am," "I was what I was," or "I will be what I will be" — an answer that includes all of time and existence.

According to ethnologists, for many people names have power and the use of the name gives the user power over the bearer of the name. It would be unthinkable for Jews to try to wield power over God, so they did not use His chief name except on the most sacred moment of the year, when they sought forgiveness.

YHVH Equals Adonai

Instead of trying to pronounce the YHVH, Jews call Him *Adonai*, which means "our Lord." When you read Scriptures in Hebrew, when you reach YHVH, you will notice that the vowels are the vowels of *Adonai*, to remind you that it is written YHVH but must be pronounced *Adonai*. This substitution of vowels is the origin of the word "Jehovah." Some ill-informed scholars took the consonants and the vowels (which were never meant to go together) and produced a hybrid word. Jehovah has a fine ring to it, but it is a sciolism, a scholar's mistake.

Elohim is another frequent name of God, it sometimes appears in shorter form, *El*. Both are translated "God." Other names include *Shaddai*, "Almighty;" *Adonai Tze-va-ot*, "Lord of Hosts;" *Melech Malchai HaMelachim*, "King of Kings;" *Ribono shel Olam*, "Master of the World;" *HaKadosh Baruch Hu*, "The Holy One, Blessed be He;" *HaMakom*, "The Place" (God is the place of the world); *HaShem*, "The Name;" *K'dosh Yisrael*, "The Holy One of Israel;" *HaRachaman*, "The Merciful One."

Each Name Has a Meaning of Its Own

Why so many names? The rabbis said that each name represented one attribute of God and so we needed many even to begin to represent Him. One meant the Merciful, another the Judge, a third the All-Powerful, etc. Also, we think that some of these ancient names came from different ages or perhaps from different tribes or areas of the Jewish people. The people developed names which seemed most meaningful to them.

5

God versus G-d

Traditional Jews to this day will not write or speak God's name except in formal prayer. Even when *Adonai* is used as a substitute for YHVH, they will say *Adoshem* or *HaShem*, substituting variants of the word "the Name." They say that *Adonai* too is a holy name and must not be taken in vain. Traditional Jews will not write out the word "God" or "Lord," substituting "G-d" or "L-rd" — as otherwise they could not dispose of the paper they wrote on as it contains the divine name. This is all part of the eternal reverence they hold is necessary in addressing, speaking of, or even writing of God.

Is God more in one place than another?

We hold that God's presence is throughout the world. There is no place we can go to avoid God. Yet the rabbis thought that God could be in one place more than in another. When people study the Torah, when people eat together and then thank Him and bless His name, there, the rabbis said, God's presence is greater. When people do deeds of loving-kindness, they express God's will and so we may say that His presence is there.

There is the wonderful story of the two brothers who each wanted to help the other. At harvest time, each took a sack of grain from his own store to give to his brother as an act of love. The spot where they met was so filled with God's presence that the old legend says that He decided the Temple would be built there.

It is man's holiness which makes a place holy, not anything inherent in the spot. Judaism pointed out that the holiness of a place lasts only as long as the act of holiness lasts. We do not know where Moses saw the burning bush. We are not sure which mountain is Mt. Sinai; our ancestors never bothered to mark it. God did not let the Israelites know where Moses was buried lest they turn his grave into a shrine.

There are tombs which the credulous treat as shrines, the Cave of the Machpelah in Hebron, where Abraham, Isaac and Jacob are supposed to be buried. The tomb of Rachel, just outside Bethlehem, which is a shrine to which barren women come to supplicate. The tomb of David on Mt. Zion is almost certainly a medieval tomb of some worthy which was mistaken for that of the great king.

The Western Wall

The holiest site for modern Jews is the Western or Wailing Wall in Jerusalem, and many throng there to pray. The Temple stood right above it 1900 years ago. Yet no one would say that a prayer spoken in our own synagogue is of less merit than the same prayer spoken at the Wall. The great expanse above the Wall where the Temple stood is off limits to traditional Jews, as they aver its ancient holiness clings to it. Liberal and Conservative Jews do ascend the Temple mount, though it is with an awareness of the site's focal place in Jewish history. Yet we would not say that God's presence is necessarily greater there than any place else.

People and their actions are the material of holiness. Deeds of loving-kindness, study, prayer — these bring God's blessing. The land of Israel is called the Holy Land, but an evil deed there is just as evil as one done any place else.

The Shechina

The rabbis said that if people did deeds of goodness, or studied, or prayed with fervor, God's presence would rest on them. This presence is called the *shechina*. It is not a separate being at all. It is as though there were more of God in that place. Just as the sun's rays fall equally over a terrain, but in places the rays seem even warmer, more concentrated, so it is with God's presence. He responds when man has brought holiness into being.

Was the world created by God, or by some natural, scientific accident, as some scientists suppose?

Judaism has traditionally taught that God created the world. The first chapters of Genesis are our ancestors' understanding of cosmogony, creation. Their version has profound religious and ethical insights, but it never was intended as a logical, scientific explanation.

That we believe that the world evolved through many eons of time is not a contradiction of the Biblical account of creation. Many have said that the Torah states the same thing poetically. Only the ultra-Orthodox today maintain that the world was made in six ordinary days. That we do not agree with them does not alter our belief in Judaism. One can be a faithful Jew and yet concur with Darwin.

We believe that the physical laws of the universe did not happen by chance. The whole idea of the universe is not just random chance; there is an intelligence behind the formulating of the cosmos. This intelligence desired to create the world. We call it God.

Physical and Spiritual Law

Harlow Shapley, the Harvard astronomer, said that there must be a hundred million inhabited planets in the cosmos. It is likely that some have reached higher forms of life than we have. Dr. Shapley was asked by a rabbi, "Do the physical laws of science hold true there too?" He answered, "From all we know, they do." The rabbi retorted, "We believe the spiritual laws that we know hold true there too." There is no contradiction between Dr. Shapley's postulation and Judaism.

Science attempts to explain how the universe came into being and how it exists. Each time a scientific breakthrough is achieved new theories evolve. Science has provided no immutable explanations. New scientific challenges abound. This is the strength of science. Judaism's purpose is different. Judaism attempts to deal with the meaning of our lives and with the God-like possibilities within us and our society. There is no incompatibility between the physical and the spiritual worlds. Religion's purpose is to explain why and how we should live to make our lives and the universe meaningful.

Does God control everything that happens?

This is the question that defeated the growth of Islam. Until the end of the Middle Ages the Arabs had the most advanced culture in the world. But they began to place great emphasis on theology and it soon affected their whole concept of being. They reasoned: "God is perfect. He must know everything, past, present and future. God is all-powerful and therefore He must control everything. Man is God's creature and does as He has determined." Everything is predetermined in God's mind and is according to His will. Man cannot have free will. What seems evil or ugly is according to God's will and must be accepted. The only time man must rise up and protest is when someone blasphemes God, for it is a test to see if man is faithful.

This Arab theology means that since everything is God's and according to His will, nothing man can do can change anything — nor should man want to change anything. Within a brief time Islam settled into a mental and physical torpor from which it is only now emerging.

Man Has Free Will

Judaism avers that God is all-knowing, and yet man has complete free will. It is man who creates poverty or slums or war, not God. So too it is man who clears slums and relieves poverty and makes peace. The evil deeds are against God's laws; the good deeds are in accord with His teachings. God permits the evil, but lets us know that we are punished for creating and allowing evil. God assists those who try to abolish poverty or war, and we find blessing and bring blessing to others in acting well.

Judaism says that although God does not control everything that happens — by His own decision, for otherwise man would be a puppet and could not be free — God does control the way the world exists. Just as the laws of physics are immutable, so God has established not only the laws of nature, but the interrelationships between all living beings.

To say that God controls the sparrow's fall is a poetic image, but it expresses a meaning beyond poetry. It means that all of creation is related, that the sparrow's death or its birth affect the world about it — and as such every other living thing. Sparrows or men, we are all ultimately related. What each person does affects others in an unending chain.

All life is God's. He does not control us; we live freely. But we are interrelated, to Him, to every other person. This relationship was established by God just as firmly as is all creation.

Does God punish people when they do something wrong?

We do not believe that God is an eternal policeman who watches every action and then rushes in to punish. The Bible speaks of God as "slow to anger."

Yet we do know that punishment does come if our actions demand it. A person who has no regard for his health, drinks too much liquor, smokes, or takes drugs will become seriously ill; can he then say God punishes him? A person who gets angry readily loses friends, loses his family's love; can he blame God? A person who refuses to study is doomed to leading a life without achievement; can he say God is punishing him? A person who does not learn to pray loses his closeness to God and the warmth of the congregation; is it God who punishes? Or is it the natural result of cause and effect, that bad deeds performed or good deeds unperformed produce unfortunate results?

So too, nations which are cruel to other nations usually are cruel to their own people, and in the end they are defeated. National policies which are shortsighted usually end with hurting the people who made them as much as the people they caused to suffer. An example would be the terrible treatment of the blacks in this country. The blacks suffered the most, but the country as a whole was seriously weakened and hurt by the stupidity of bigotry. It was not God who punished the whites who were prejudiced. The bigotry cut both ways.

This is our understanding, that God does not "punish," but He fashioned the world so that evil does produce evil, as good produces good.

Accident, Injury and Death

Sometimes the punishment seems greater than the "guilt" of the punished person. If a child runs into the street and is struck by an auto, his punishment for a moment's indiscretion may be fatal. But can we blame God for punishing him? Everyone weeps as it is a tragedy, but it is not punishment that is involved. It is a simple fact that autos can be involved in fatal accidents, and we must learn to be careful or we suffer.

So we say that God does not punish in the sense that it is His decree that the child be hit by a car, that the man who smokes should develop a dreadful disease, or any of these things. We bring the punishment upon ourselves.

Sometimes, alas, the innocent suffer for the stupidities of others. A drunken driver may collide with another car and kill its innocent occupants. The son or daughter of a man who smokes or drinks too much and so dies early will grow up orphaned and poor. Again, it is not punishment. We are involved with other people, attached to them. No one, not even a hermit, lives alone, for we are all entangled in the lives and destinies of others, of the community, of the world.

Personal Guilt

In the personal realm of *mitzvah*, commandment or good deed, and *aveira*, sin or evil deed, we do not feel that God rushes in to punish just because we do not always live up to our duties as Jews. Judaism does want each of us to do well, to be worthy of being a Jew. But it does not want us to go about feeling guilty.

This is why we rejoice when Yom Kippur is over. We feel that God does not want to punish. He wants us to turn from our evil deeds, to do good. Does He reward? Yes, often, with the feeling of goodness done, of virtue achieved.

Is God really testing the Jews with such events as the Holocaust?

At one time the idea that man had to be tested to see if his faith was certain seemed important. This idea is explicit in Abraham's belief that God demanded that he sacrifice Isaac on Mount Moriah. Later rabbis tried to say that Abraham misunderstood God's command, that he only wanted Abraham to worship on the spot where the Temple would stand, Modern scholars maintain that this was God's dramatic way of showing that he refused human sacrifices, and as such was a huge cultural and religious step forward.

Yet tradition holds that the sounding of the shofar of Rosh Hashanah is supposedly a reminder of Abraham's and Isaac's faith and willingness to endure the sacrifice, and so serves as an instrument of forgiveness to the Jews of today. There is an old rabbinic phrase, *z'chut avot*, the "merit of the fathers," which implies that Abraham's and Isaac's strength of faith serves as a help to their descendants today. Modern rabbis preach that the blowing of the shofar is a reminder to us to emulate their faithfulness.

Most Jewish thinkers today do not consider the Holocaust or any other grave persecution as a test of Israel's faith. Most of us would refuse the question entirely. The six million who died were not being tested. What kind of God do we believe in if He could allow six million to be slain to test the rest of us? Perhaps Abraham was being tested, but Isaac was not sacrificed.

Modern Jewish thinkers consider the Holocaust an outcome of man's perfidy. When evil men are allowed to seize power, the innocent are the first to suffer. That Hitler selected the Jews as his prime target was not God's doing. It was an evil man lashing out at the people who had brought God's ways to mankind. In rejecting God, in rejecting the Ten Commandments, Hitler rejected the people who gave these to the world's comprehension and vented his mad anger on them.

A Test of God

Yet there are thinkers today who use the Holocaust as a test. Richard Rubenstein uses it as a test of God. He maintains that it is impossible to believe in God after Auschwitz.

The Lubavitcher Rebbe, whose movement lost half of its members to the Nazis, declared that the Holocaust was exactly the kind of test Abraham was subjected to, and as Abraham and his descendants were rewarded for their fidelity, so Jews today will find such a reward. Indeed, there are some who claim that the reward is manifest, that the state of Israel was established because the Jewish people were proved in the crucible of history. A high price, many of us would say.

The Test of History

Professor Emil Fackenheim poses the problem differently, as befits the rabbi and philosopher he is. He says that whether God was testing us or not, history was. If we who remain give up on God and Judaism, Hitler will have won long after his body was burned in his Berlin bunker.

What the Holocaust did demonstrate is that the truths of the Torah are alive today, both in their blessings and in their warnings. We are told in Deuteronomy and in the books of the prophets how man brings retribution upon himself and upon the world when he creates evil or when he allows evil to exist. Evil gives birth to evil, and it becomes a living force, burning, tearing, destroying. Good gives birth to good, bringing blessings without number. This is faith, and this is our deep understanding and conviction.

Why doesn't God speak to people today?

The rabbis have always maintained that God speaks to all generations, including our own.

At first God spoke to patriarchs, and then to Moses and Aaron. Afterwards He spoke to the prophets. But Judaism says that He continued to speak to the people of Israel through the great sages of the Talmud. The great difference is that God seems to have spoken directly to the prophets, but in later generations He spoke "through" the rabbis. In Biblical days His voice was clear and direct. Later, the voice was muted in the sense that those who were moved to speak and to teach did not feel themselves as spokesmen for God, but rather as spokesmen for an inspired tradition. The combination of wisdom and spirit brought forth teachings that added to our heritage and which to the Orthodox are equal in validity to the teachings of the Torah itself.

The Prophets Disappear

Why did the form of God's inspiration change? The major difficulty was the determining who is a true prophet and who is fraudulent or self-deceived. When men would claim that God was speaking directly through them, there was no way of checking except through the pragmatic: did it make sense? did it work for the individual or the people? Time alone could demonstrate whether the voice was truly God's. The only practical immediate test was to try to see whether the prophesies were positive or destructive.

But the perspectives were too short, and by the time of the third century before the common era the people found they could no longer depend on any checks and so refused all claimants to the mantle of prophesy. This is a major reason why the various books of the Apocrypha and Pseudepigrapha, though written by and for Jews, were barred from the canon of the Bible.

The Rabbis Speak for God

Instead a new way of finding inspiration and instruction came into being.

The teachings of the rabbis were accepted as both inspired by God and binding on the people. As the innovators were the actual teachers of tradition, there was no longer worry as to whether their messages were fraudulent or destructive.

This concept found Biblical buttressing. In the great covenant made with the Israelites after the completion of their forty-year wandering in Sinai, they were told that the commandment of God "is not hidden from you, nor is it far off" (Deut. 30:11). It is not in heaven any more, nor is it beyond the sea, "but the word is very near to you, in your mouth, and in your heart, that you may do it" (v. 14). So the Jews reasoned that their own understanding had God's blessing, and they would find His inspiration in diligent study and search for His truths.

Since the era of the Talmud we believe that God speaks to man in many ways, through the great and wise men of every generation. Not only to the Jews, but to all great men does He speak. The charge to our ancestors to find God's word operating among mankind is still alive with us today. It is our job to acquire wisdom, to seek holiness, and thus become capable of hearing God in our own lives.

If a person devotes himself to being a good Jew and tries to have a personal relationship with God, how does he know if God responds?

Some people thought they had a clear answer to this problem. They found in the Bible the passages which speak of how we earn God's blessing or His curse (Deut. 28). So, they reasoned, if they lived in peace and prosperity God was blessing them because they were living lives pleasing unto Him. If other people suffered war or poverty, these were signs that God was cursing them because He disapproved of their lives.

This philosophy is pleasant to the man who is rich and at ease, but it is scarcely consoling to the man beset by troubles. A long time ago the prophets noticed a vital discrepancy in such a simplistic answer to our question. They saw the Babylonians sitting on top of the world while the Jews were beaten and dispersed. In no way could anyone imagine that the cruel, pagan Babylonians deserved God's blessings. The Jews at their worst were better ethically and spiritually than their oppressors. The book of Job too pointed out that the good and innocent may suffer and it would be wrong to attribute their condition to God's curse or displeasure.

Through the centuries the Jews have lived under oppression of the medieval church and later the modern nation behemoths of Germany and Russia, and there are few who would hold that these tyrannies deserved God's blessing more than the Jews they oppressed.

State of Grace

Some branches of Christianity believe that their followers can be conscious of being in a condition where they are blessed by God. This is termed the "state of grace." Pronounced and affirmed by the church, the state of grace achieved by the communicant is proof positive that he is living according to the teachings of his church and has thus earned God's blessing.

Judaism does not allow that such a state of grace exists. There is no condition in Judaism that clearly indicates that God is definitely pleased with us. There are prescribed religious and ethical duties, but no Jew would dare claim that he has satisfied them all. The obligations are infinite. For instance, there are blessings for many actions in Judaism — washing, eating, lighting Sabbath candles — yet there are no blessings to be recited for doing a good deed, giving to charity, or honoring one's parents. The rabbis said that this is because no person can do enough good deeds, no person can honor his parents sufficiently. There can be no complete discharge of the duties incumbent on man.

In Judaism there is no stasis, a reaching of a desired point and remaining in this state. We say that all living is striving. The blessing is in the striving even more than in the attaining.

A Personal Relationship

There is another aspect of this question, the idea of an individual reaching a personal relationship with God. This can be on a low level, such as Tevye's conversations with God in the Sholem Aleichem stories. It can be on a high level, as in the Hasidic *tzaddiks'* mystical experiences, to them true encounters with God.

Generally, Judaism's approach is that personal experience with God is possible, but only with great circumspection and always with the rational mind involved. No drugs or liquor or other artificial aids are countenanced, only prayer, meditation and, sometimes, fasting. Most important, the response must be positive. God's message must be creative and in accord with Judaism's ethical and ritual teachings. The way of discerning a false prophet is by the destructive message he offers (Deut. 13:1-5).

The final answer is that of faith. We cannot be sure that our actions are truly pleasing to God. Even the supposition seems presumptuous. Yet we cannot go ahead in life unless we feel that we are somehow on the right road. We do our utmost, and trust that He will respond.

Why do some people not believe in God?

Some people make up their minds and refuse to think further, despite any argumentation or "proof." This applies to religious people and nonreligious people alike. There is a league of Christian fundamentalists who maintain the world is flat, and any proof that it is round to them is blasphemous. Conversely, the Soviet government officially maintains there is no God and any Soviet citizen who is religious is considered a threat to the state. Soviet publications insist on spelling the word "God" with a small "g" as official policy.

A person who is not sure whether God exists is termed an agnostic; one who firmly says there is no God is an atheist. The agnostic's position is a very comfortable one. It entails no responsibility; he reserves judgment. The atheist's position is hard to defend, as it is impossible to prove there is no God.

Years ago Robert Ingersoll, a prominent atheist, would stand before an audience with his watch in his hand. He would give God five minutes to smite him dead. When the thunderbolt did not materialize, Ingersoll would proudly state that he had proved God does not exist.

Most "proofs" are on this ridiculous level. Most of the denials of God seem to be a matter of emotion. Freud said that he never met a Jew who denied his religion who did not hate his father – for the parent and God the Father would merge emotionally and be rejected simultaneously.

The Soul's Failure

Some people are deaf to music. Others see no harmony in art. Some people cannot make friends. Just so, some people are deaf or blind or dumb to the idea of God. They cannot feel the outreach of their own spirit. They cannot detect it in others.

To the person who is willing to look and evaluate the evidence, there seem to be great answers in the structure of the universe, in the logical and emotional nature of man, in the existence of the world of ideas, of structural harmony, of beauty, of bravery and sacrifice and dedication.

To deny that these are the products of a divine intelligence and to insist that they just happened by themselves is to presuppose a miracle far more difficult to believe than anything mentioned in Holy Scriptures.

Without the idea of God, all of cosmos is an accident of matter and energy and time and therefore as meaningless as any accident or coincidence. With the concept of God, the cosmos takes on celestial meaning, all part of a planned universe.

Alas, there are people who are willing to judge the creation of the universe in personal terms. They feel themselves the sole arbiters. It is an indication of the puniness of some men's minds and the *chutzpah* of defining the world in terms of their own limited knowledge and evolution.

God as Meaning of the Universe

Without God nothing would mean anything — life, love, family, country. Everything would be just a joining of atoms in haphazard union, for there would be no reason for anything coming together or ever being. Without God even a single amoeba is fantastic. With God all takes on meaning. Love is love, sacrifice is meaningful, thoughts and ideas and achievements have permanence in the frame of time. Life and death count.

We believe that life and spirit are not futile, they have significance. Life without God is less than a dream in the night, a cruel consciousness that can bring only despair to the thinking. With God, it is an awakening to responsibility and to glory.

What is faith?

Faith in Judaism is far more than the words, "I believe in God." Faith is the assurance that God loves man and is concerned for us. There is a huge difference between saying God exists and believing in Him. We can say we believe in God only when the fact of His existence has such compelling meaning that it affects the quality of our lives. Faith must be a living and dynamic component of our lives, if we are to claim that we are believers in God.

In the Bible

Faith has been essential in Judaism since its inception, yet the word is not mentioned in the Torah even once. The prophets understood it to be basic to Jewish living. "If you have no faith, you shall not be established" (Isaiah 7:9).

The matter of faith was rarely alluded to by the rabbis of the Talmud. Usually faith in God was so fundamental to their understanding that there were no questions asked so there were none to answer. There is one Midrash which sets the tone of Jewish faith. After the crossing of the Sea of Reeds, we have the great Song of the Sea. Rabbi Abahu said, "When Israel gained faith, then they could sing" (Ex. Rabba 23:2).

Neither Midrash nor Talmud offers a definition of *emunah*, of faith; it is simply assumed. The Jew had faith in God and His Torah. There was a natural linking of God, the Torah, and man — man who covenanted with God and lived by the commandments of His Torah.

To Be Firm

The Hebrew root of *emunah* is *a-m-n*, the same as in the word *amen*. It means "to be firm," "to make firm," "to hold fast." It is used in the building trade in the sense of "to construct," "to make fast or firm." From this root come *aman*, "master workman" or "artist;" *uman*, "mechanic;" *omnah*, "pillar," that which holds up a roof and makes it firm.

According to the lexicon, the word's prime root is based on a homely action, "holding a child in one's arms, the firmness that comes from being carried by a mother or father." This is the origin of the meaning, *aman*, "nurse."

The spiritual overtones of *emunah* come from its meaning to be firm, to be steadfast, dependable and consistent — to be faithful. *Amen*, the word that closes every *beracha*, blessing, does not mean "may it be so!" — this would indicate that our faith is only great enough to hope that the *beracha* is true or to be fulfilled. *Amen* is an experience of faith, that it *is* so. Otherwise saying *amen* after the blessing over wine or bread would be a strange thing. Bread or wine is before us. We bless God for creating it. This is not a hope for the future. It is fact.

When we close a prayer rather than a blessing with *amen*, it does not only mean that we hope the prayer will be fulfilled. This we cannot know, though our faith tells us that God will respond. The *amen* at the close of a petitionary prayer is to acknowledge that we have addressed a living God, who does respond. What He does to us or for us is up to Him; the *amen* is an expression of faith, not just of hope.

Emunah then, the faith of man in God, is like the confidence a child feels in the arms of his parents, the sense of security, safety, of warmth. Such faith is not destroyed by suffering or pain. It is based on confidence and love which outlast any disruption, any separation.

A Faith That Is Aware

Nor is *emunah* blind faith, though it is a reliance on Him who is unseen. *Emunah* is based on continuing revelation emanating from the God "who renews the miracles of creation each day" (Siddur).

The Jew stands before God in the strength of his piety, with faith that he may acquire merit in the face of the Divine.

If Judaism is all reason, why is there need for faith? We cannot arrive at all of God's truth by use of our minds. If we could, no one would have doubts. We reach God through faith. The soul divines that which it seeks, said Plato. Our intelligence interprets what we have discovered through faith. (My thanks to Rabbi Robert I. Kahn, for his article "Amen," *Dimensions, Winter 1970.)*

Is there an official Jewish theology comparable to that of Thomas Aquinas in the Roman Catholic Church?

No, there never has been. The lack of a formal creed or theology sets Judaism apart from Christianity and the way traditional Christianity thinks and functions. Ever since the Nicene Council of 325 C.E., there has been a creed which is still official for most of the Christian world.

In the 13th century Thomas Aquinas, in his *Summa Theologiae*, set the philosophic and theologic bases of Roman Catholicism. In it he attempted to reconcile Aristotelian philosophy with Christian faith. The philosophy helped give form to the expression of faith. Actually the theories of Duns Scotus, who was a Platonist, prevail now, but the thought system of Aquinas has been the undergirding of Catholicism since his day.

Judaism possesses a somewhat similar thought system in that of Maimonides, who a century earlier than Aquinas attempted to reconcile Judaism with Aristotelianism. Neither Maimonides nor any other Jewish theologian was able to impose a theological system on Judaism, which was already three thousand years old in his day. A major reason for the basic unity of the Jewish people and religion is indeed the refusal of a formal philosophic or theologic system. Nobody could impose such a system on Judaism, so there never was need to rebel against one.

The emphasis in Judaism has ever been on deed and study, learning what the *mitzvot* are, what are God's commandments, from the Torah and the Talmud—and practicing these *mitzvot.* Philosophy of theology or even interpretation of faith was usually considered extraneous to the life of the Jew.

What Does God Want?

"Know before Whom you stand!" (Berachot 28b) is inscribed on the walls of many synagogues. It is interpreted as "Know what God wants you to do in your life!" Because Jews live over most of the globe, there are variations in the worship service and in customs and usage. But as long as all Jews hold the performance of the *mitzvot* as the test of the pious Jew, no schism can arise from theological differences. The Karaites did produce a schism when they denied the authority of the Talmud and the *mitzvot* derived from the Talmud.

Even such a seeming break in Judaism as the Hasidic movement ended with the Hasidim becoming the most Orthodox of all. In two generations they moved from a kind of reform to full adherence to all the *mitzvot* and the utmost of concern in the study of Talmud and its commentaries.

Jewish theological writings of the Middle Ages and of recent years were more a reaction to the intellectual climate than born of an inner need. Maimonides' "Guide to the Perplexed" is considered the supreme expression of Jewish theology, yet it has never been accepted by any formal body, and it has been rejected by many rabbis. Recent attempts at a theologically comprehensive treatment of Judaism never were meant to impose an ideology on Jews or Judaism. They were meant rather to explain Judaism to Jews and non-Jews alike. Judaism will long outlast its theologians.

What is the nature of man?

Jewish tradition states that man is basically good, as he was created in the image of God. Indeed, the rabbis said that God's purpose in creating man was the good deeds that he envisioned man performing. (Gen. Rabba 8). Like God, man has the power to discern and to choose, to say yes or no. He is born with freedom of will, but this necessitates his being able to say no to the good. He is born with the capacity to choose evil, so he may turn out to be evil—and he is usually a compound of good and evil. Our prayerbook says there is no man who does not commit evil. Yet only the most depraved of men will not be moved to compassion at some time in their lives.

Man therefore is a composite. He is wise and he is foolish; he can love and he can hate; build and destroy; conceive great visions and yet allow slums and prejudice and pollution. He can sacrifice himself for great ideals, and can be deluded so as to sacrifice himself to defend a totalitarian dictatorship.

Man has the capacity to grow, to learn from his experience, and what is uniquely human, to learn from the experience of others, through their counsel or by report.

The Soul Is Born Pure

Man can do evil, but he can also atone and learn to do good. Man is not born with a taint on his soul, as Christianity terms it, original sin. Each person is born free. "The soul which Thou hast given me came pure from Thee," reads the *siddur*. It must be nourished to grow as much as must the body. It can flower into greatness and produce splendor. It can be crushed, and soulless men are evil incarnate. The purpose of Judaism, indeed, of all higher religions, is to enable the soul to grow so that man may refrain from evil and do that which is good.

Although there are more negative than positive *mitzvot*, 365 to 248, in the reckoning of the Talmud's 613 commandments, the rabbis said that refraining from doing evil is never enough; a person must do good actively as well. They added that the reward for doing good is far more than the reward for refraining from evil. Man's nature is such, they felt, that most men respond to the idea of doing positive good rather than to the threat of punishment for sinning.

Judaism carries this idea even further. It speaks of man's inner compulsion to build a better world. Human beings have the incredible privilege of being partners with God in building a world of human dignity, brotherhood and spiritual attainment (Shabbat 119b). All humans are free to choose. If they choose wisely they have an intrinsic role to play in the fulfillment of God's grand design for the world.

Does Judaism provide a sure heaven to those who practice it faithfully?

Abraham was a particularly courageous man. Not only did he embrace a faith in an invisible God, which was sufficient to earn him the enmity of every king and priest of his day—for in every early civilization the religion was a state religion and part of the polity—he also projected a faith without "surety." In some ways this took even more courage than to defy king and priest or to believe in one God who is invisible.

Pagan faiths had developed systems that provided just this surety. The priests instituted sacrifices and rituals which were "guaranteed" to satisfy the gods or other powers. The proper sacrifices accompanied by the necessary rites with the needed gifts to the shrine and its priests were considered absolute in placating the gods.

The Egyptians developed elaborate ritual and ceremonies to accompany mummification, which assured everlasting life. The most primitive and the most advanced civilizations of the ancient world were united in this one premise: their priests knew the proper path to immortality. Ideas of morality played little part in determining whether the individual was worthy of immortality. The ceremonies rigidly adhered to were the essential, and no one who could afford to pay for them had to fear extinction or undue punishment in the afterlife.

The Many Mitzvot

From the first, Judaism would not be satisfied with ritual and ceremony. Abraham recognized that God demanded justice and deeds of loving-kindness. And deeds of loving-kindness cannot be measured precisely. God gave the commandments, not just the Decalog, but also the 613 of the Torah, to which custom and the rabbis added until their number is beyond exact calculation. No person can satisfy them all, even the most Orthodox.

Some scholars believe that the commandments were proliferated to answer this problem of how we can measure the amount of adherence to God's law that will earn God's love. By presenting man with such a great measure of *halachah*, of God's laws, the rabbis could say that the Jew spent his days walking (the root word of *halachah*) in the paths of God, the paths God Himself had set for those who would obey Him.

No matter how important *halachah* is, most of us would agree that the overwhelming impulse of Judaism is to deeds of loving-kindness. Assuredly deeds of loving-kindness are mankind's faith in God expressed in action.

They are considered man's highest response to the loving-kindness of God. Yet no one, not the paragon of all virtues, would dare say he had honestly satisfied God's demand on him. What individual has honored his parents enough, or has loved his neighbor wholeheartedly, or has helped the downtrodden sufficiently? Even intimating that he has done so would be proof of either hubris or insensitivity.

The rabbis were aware of this of course. They asked why there are *berachot* (blessings) for washing one's hands or breaking bread, but none for giving charity or honoring one's parents. They answered by saying that we can recognize that we have washed or have eaten, but we can never be sure that we have satisfied the *mitzvah* of loving-kindness—there is always so very much more that we might do.

This means that Judaism does not possess the certainty that other religions maintain they do. A Roman Catholic who has regularly gone to confession and mass, who has received last rites, is assured by his religion that he will be accepted in heaven. He may have to spend some period in purgatory because of lapses in his confessions, but final salvation will be his.

The Path with a Goal

Judaism does not offer this surety of redemption. Some Orthodox Jews feel that the performance of the *mitzvot* with *kavana* (dedication), is fairly sure to win God's approval, for they feel the path of *halachah* is the path that leads to God's approbation. Yet even the ultra-Orthodox recognize that the *mitzvot* alone are not enough. There is the wry story of the Jew who performed all the *mitzvot* but did not enjoy doing them. He went to paradise— but he didn't enjoy paradise either.

Judaism has always decried the service of God in hope of reward or from fear of punishment. There is the story of the woman who went about with a fire in an earthenwear jar and a jug of water. The water was to quench hell; the fire to burn down paradise. Her intent: to force man to serve God only from love, not from fear or hope of reward.

This is the noble intent which underlies Judaism's cardinal idea. We do not serve God except from respect, honor and love. This is mature religion. Alas, it brings us back to our first point. We cannot know whether we have ever done enough to satisfy God's demands on us. The reward for studying Torah is in the studying. The reward for doing deeds of loving-kindness is in the doing. The reward for being a good person, a good Jew, is in the being. More than this we cannot ask. But we do have faith in God. This is our trust.

Why is there killing, war, poverty, slavery, hunger?

The world grows, not straight but slowly and crookedly. We call this growth "evolution." We believe that man is the product of God working through nature. Man has the highest gifts: spirit, intelligence, loyalty, the capacity to grow. He has the stuff of his animal past: cruelty, savagery. Indeed, he is sometimes a superpredator, far more destructive than any animal. He has also added the lust for power and wealth.

The Pretty Answer

Judaism like the other great religions wants man to outgrow his animal origins, but he learns ever so slowly. He makes progress in science and industry more readily than in morality. Yet there is progress. Slavery has almost disappeared. Even in Arab lands, there is little at long last. In a few countries there is little real poverty.

Judaism says the evils of war, of crime, of poverty are man-made and not God-made. Man can end killing by outlawing war, when men "shall beat their swords into plowshares" (Isaiah 2 & Micah 4). The Hebrew word *shalom* has an even wider meaning than the word "peace," for it signifies welfare of every kind, security, contentment, friendship.

Much more must be done to banish evil from our midst—and each of us must recognize his duty to aid. So the answer to this question is not an answer in words. Our response must be commitment and action.

Reality

This is a pretty answer, but it begs the question. The answer is not that simple. Until a few decades ago most liberal theologians described the world as a product of evolution with a definite sense of progress, of goals attainable, of dreams realizable. The few preachers of doom were excoriated as lacking faith. Man and the world were perfectible.

Since Hitler and Stalin we recognize how Pollyannish we were. Our desires dictated our theology. Any presentation today that is not cognizant of the beast that lurks in man, of the gross inequities of the world of men, of war, poverty, famine and disease, is not only guilty of whitewash but is criminally guilty—for theology *sans* truth is false and criminal.

Wars persist and they kill with the contrivance of modern technology. That we have outgrown slavery but permit Harlem or Watts to exist is little cause for self-congratulation. Crops that rot in the field or in silos while millions starve, the bigotry of God-fearing *apartheid* practitioners, men who sell heroin to children, all are an affront to God and our understanding.

God does not cause these horrors. Man does. It is man who will have to grow to the maturity he claims for himself in at least some areas. Yet how does a perfect God permit these things?

The Solution

The question of evil and a perfect God has plagued thinking man for eons. The books of Job and Ecclesiastes are directed to just this question. Both end in saying that man's mind is not great enough to encompass the problem, that God moves in mysterious ways.

Orthodox Judaism says that evil is God's way to test man, to discipline man, to punish man. It is we who are imperfect, and His perfection is unassailable. These answers have satisfied and do satisfy millions, and we must respect those who accept them. Some of us must seek further.

A Solution

In the Talmud man is termed God's partner in the finishing of the creation of the universe (Shabbat 10a). If God needs a partner, is He indeed perfect? Some of us will say yes, that He has given of His power to man by His own will, and allowed man the responsibility of completing the world as a divine challenge. It is much as though a great painter sketched in the forms of a mural and then directed his apprentices to complete the rest. This is the classical Reform position.

There are some thinking people who say that God Himself is growing, that he needs man to complete His growth as well as that of the world. The medieval philosophers spoke of *tzim-tzum,* that God deliberately diminished Himself and His reign so that man would have room in which to act freely. Modern thinkers hold that God works slowly through evolution because this is His nature, and that He and the world can only be completed through natural growth and the will to reach perfection.

God without man to help Him is deprived of His sons' aid. God and man together are needed to complete the work, and if His children do not assist, they are unfaithful to Him and harmful to themselves.

This concept of an incomplete God, a growing God, may annoy some people, and yet it is a cogent answer to the grave questions of evil in a world created by God. God is still the creator, the director, the guide to all of us. His is still the spirit that animates and ennobles. We must become creators, animators, partners with Him to finish, to ennoble—the world and ourselves.

The rabbis said that God always provides the cure for any affliction. The cure for the evil of the world is the Torah (Kiddushin 30a). Go and apply it.

According to tradition any Jewish law may be broken to save a life or in dire emergency except three: one may not murder, perform idolatry, or commit incest or adultery. Why were these three excepted?

At a very early date our ancestors realized that God's commandments were given to enhance life, not to rob man of life or its meaning. So they decided that almost any religious law would be suspended in order to save a life or to relieve great anguish. The rabbis confirmed the above three categories in the Talmud. Though a man holds a dagger to your chest and commands that you kill another person, Judaism says you may not, not even at the cost of your own life. You may not destroy an innocent life to save your own.

Idolatry removes meaning from life. It reduces life to an impious fraud. Holiness becomes a mockery. As God does not exist in idolatry and life is ruled by the stern government of implacable fate or by the capricious rule of gods or miracle-working beings, there is neither reason nor justice. Good and evil are equally nonsensical. Man's deeds and his prayers are both of no value as fate cannot be affected by anything man does, and the capricious gods work according to their own wills. Judaism denies that man is governed by fate or that there are gods or spirits that control man's destiny. Judaism says that there is reason in the universe, there is goodness just as there is evil. Remove the distinction between God and the gods and you have removed the very reason for life and the world.

Love Is Holy

Adultery and incest were to the Jew the nadir of human experience. A person who could indulge in either was assumed to be below human standards. They demonstrate an utter disregard for love, for devotion, for family loyalty and purity. They demean the human to the level of an animal. According to traditional Judaism even the most solemn atonement can never truly expunge these grave sins. If life does not have ethical standards, its norms for human conduct, then life has no value. The pagan cults indulged in just these debaucheries which turned men and women into beasts.

Life must have value, and so the rabbis established these three categories which cannot be breached lest all life become rubbish.

Orthodox Jews observe every aspect of *halachah*, **Jewish law, each** *mitzvah*, **commandment. If man is supposedly free before God, how can he be forced to observe** *halachah*? **May he not make up his own mind?**

The rabbis asked, "Who has the greater merit, the man who does a *mitzvah* because he is enjoined to, or the man who does it of his own free will?" Their answer may surprise some people, for they held that the man who is enjoined to do the *mitzvah* gains the greater merit. He has accepted the responsibility of observing all the *mitzvot*, whereas the other man may pick and choose and accept only that which appeals to him. The Orthodox Jew avers that *halachah* is God-ordained, and he will not consider whether or not he will observe a *mitzvah*. Indeed, he is prohibited from even attempting to weigh one *mitzvah* against another, lest he decide he will perform the more important and forgo the lesser. To him each is God-ordained and must be fulfilled equally.

There are some *mitzvot* he cannot do, for they are predicated on the existence of the Temple and its cult. Yet even today *kohanim*, descendants of the priests of the Temple, may not marry a convert or a divorcee as this would prohibit their functioning in the Temple—when it is restored. Nor may they abdicate their priestly role; being born a *kohen* is irrevocable.

Spirit and Law

Reform and Conservative Jews do not accept this philosophy of Judaism. They do choose which *mitzvot* to obey and which to relinquish. They may do so according to what seems to them to be high criteria. The Orthodox Jew's response is one of severe censure. To him it means that an individual

Jew has set his own mind as the judge of the value of each *mitzvah*, preferring his own fallible reason over God's own law.

The Orthodox Jew yet maintains that he is entirely a free agent. He is not forced. He voluntarily chooses the life of an Orthodox Jew, accepting *halachah* as God's path on earth. He will point to the Liberal or Conservative Jew as proof of his own freedom, for nothing but his own decision prevents his emulating them.

The Conservative or Liberal Jew has what seem to him valid reasons for his choice of a life style, yet he cannot negate the reasoning of the traditional Jew. Each person must determine his own course, and as such find the role within Judaism that is his or her own.

We usually think of Judaism as a rational, logical religion. Yet there is a strong mystical side, the Kabbala, Zohar, modern Hasidism. How are they balanced?

Most Jews at present live with the rational logical side of Judaism foremost. In times past it was the mystical which pervaded the thinking of many if not most Jews. There is a swing from one aspect to another, and it is usually a counteraction to the position of the Jew in the world. When life is relatively good, when persecution is a minor fleabite, when a man can feel he is producing meaningfully, the rational aspects of Judaism hold sway. The great periods of mysticism seem to have been reactions to overt persecution, Hadrian, the Visigoths, the Inquisition, etc.

Most Jews through the centuries carried within them both aspects of Judaism in a kind of symbiosis. What is more, they felt no uneasiness. They lived their lives most of the time as though all was rational, but when outside forces intervened, they readily gave credence to belief in a combination of superstition and mysticism. This proclaiming a tragedy as fated (*beschert* in Yiddish) or attributing it to powers of darkness annoyed the Vilna Gaon, but he was not typical. The usual rabbi studied Talmud with all rationalism and yet contrived in the writing of *kemiyahs*, amulets, to keep away evil spirits. His daytime hours were spent in Talmud study, but in the evening he turned to mystical works.

There is a rationality in the Zohar which goes well with the logic born of Talmud study, in that it tries to systematize the metaphysics of Judaism. The nonmystic may see this as a ludicrous paradox, but this is precisely what it tries to do, to set up the *sephirot*, the essences of manifestations of God, in diagram and to explain how each works and how they interact.

One can live as a Jew with only the rational as his guide, but it means losing the thrust, the imaginative insight which is the exciting part of the mystical in Judaism. Until recently, most Jews had some of each.

The Redemption of the Cosmos

We cannot truly appreciate the meaning of the words "messiah" or "redemption" to the traditional Jew without a recognition of the immense mystical aspects of these words. Lurianic Kabbalism in the 16th and 17th centuries made of the redemption of Israel an intense cosmos-filling drama. Not only would the entire world be redeemed and the people of Israel be placed in a position of ascendancy and its teachings be the guide for all mankind to achieve a "restored world" (*olam ha-tikkun*), there would also be a supreme cosmic transformation, a fundamental change to all life and matter and to the spiritual world as well, and the rectification of the primordial catastrophe—for Adam's fall took place in heaven as well as on earth. The divine worlds as well as the earthly will be restored to their original unity and perfection.

This Kabbalistic stress on the spiritual aspects of redemption transcends even the great prophetic teachings. The preparation for the Great Day is different from the prophetic, and it is not ethical nor is it a national preparation. It is entirely an inner mystical and spiritual preparation. For mystics the anticipation of the messianic era is all-consuming. Many of the Hasidim today have precisely this dream of cosmos-wide redemption as the dream of their life and the spur of their religion. They expect the messiah's advent daily and with his coming the transformation of all inner and outer reality into the brilliance of God's supernal world. It is not surprising that their visions make them different from other Jews.

Yet Judaism contains the pointed rationalism, the logic of the Talmud, the passionate search for justice of the prophets, the dream of a better world for all mankind—and the flight to the expanse of the inexpressible and the unnamable.

Is Judaism better than other religions?

This is what lawyers call a "loaded question." If we say Judaism is better, we are accused of being immodest. If we say that it is not, then we are asked why we bother with Judaism at all.

Judaism teaches modesty. Moses is called in the Torah the most modest of men. Yet we recognize that modesty can be overdone when it becomes diffidence. A Hasidic rebbe said: The rabbis asked, "Why was the Torah given on Mt. Sinai, which is not a lofty mountain?" And they answered their question by saying, "Just because it was not high and proud." The rebbe continued, "If God wanted true modesty, why did He not give the Torah in a valley?"

His meaning is obvious: We must be aware of our own values and merits, and yet not be overbearing.

Judaism has a directness in its belief in one God and in one mankind. It is linked to the earth and the turn of the seasons, and to man's deepest needs, spiritual and emotional. It is the source of man's concept of God and of ethics. It is not based on miracles and the impossible to believe. It is rooted in history and holds life to be real and possible to change for the better. It provides the concepts by which men must live in order to achieve a meaningful life.

It provides a vehicle of prayer and aspiration that expand man's mental and moral horizons. It possesses intense beauty. It has won the love of millions of adherents through the ages, many of whom were willing to suffer to keep alive its truths. We hold it to be an inspired religion whose teachings of justice, ethics and love are contemporaneous with every age, in a society that has yet to equal Judaism's vision.

What are Jewish values?

Rabbis and teachers are always speaking about Jewish values. Are there values which Jews can claim as their own?

Jews can't claim a monopoly on any value, let alone a number of them. Yet with the years, certain values have become identified with Judaism and the Jews, though we share some of them with other people.

Certainly the Jews are not the only people who hold study a high duty, nor are Jews alone in their regard for family. Nor are Jews unique in their respect for culture, nor in their quest for peace. One could go down a long list: regard for the aged, concern for the poor, the widowed, the orphaned. The very idea of social justice as a feeling of responsibility for the community as a whole seems to be a Jewish innovation, which we would love to share with all mankind.

Few nations in ancient days had the Jewish concern for the land itself. Letting the land lie fallow every seven years was a religious restriction. The Jews with their neighbors developed terracing. The Bible speaks out against wanton destruction of trees in time of war.

The Emotions of Birds and Beasts

The Bible and the Talmud are aware of the emotions and needs of birds and beasts and sternly prohibited cruelty. One fed one's animals before he ate himself, the ox should not be muzzled as it treads out the wheat, the bird should not be taken with its eggs, the ewe or nannygoat and its lamb or kid should not be slaughtered and cooked together. The Talmud spoke of *tsaar baalei hayyim,* the emotions of everything living, and prohibited all cruelty, all wanton slaying, and derided the hunter, the man who kills for sport, as a lesser human being.

The Jews were the people of the prophets who spoke in God's name, admonishing man to act in accordance with the highest teachings. Their religion wed monotheism to ethics and stoutly maintained—as we do to this day—that true worship cannot be divorced from ethical living.

The Dignity of Life

Perhaps the highest Jewish value is the respect for the dignity of life of every human being, the recognition of the godhead within every person, of every one's being our brother, as God is father of all. These values arise from the teachings of the Torah, the prophets and the rabbis, plus the experience of living as a people for 4000 years.

A modern Jewish scholar wrote: "We would like our children to know that if they burn with righteous indignation, if they have the true feeling of brotherhood, if they place humanity high in their scale of values, if they despise hypocrisy, if they are impatient with poverty and corruption, if they are frantic at the slow pace of social reform and the complacency of their elders, at such times let them know they are in the company of Amos, Hosea, Jeremiah and Isaiah."—Rabbi Sheldon Blank.

Is there anything in Judaism like Kierkegaard's "leap of faith"?

The 19th century Danish theologian is termed the father of existentialism. He called for a faith that proceeds directly from the need of the individual's existence, and he refused to rely on tradition or the experience of others—and he denied the validity of "revealed religion." The revelation had come to another person. It was not part of his own experience or his own existence, and so Kierkegaard could not accept it for himself. Yet he recognized that rationalism could go only so far: "God does not exist; God is eternal," is the way he expressed it.

Man must use logic, he said, but death stares at man. Man does not have eternity to quibble or to amass his evidence. Finally, *in extremis*, in the extremity of his own need, Kierkegaard took the "leap of faith" - trusting that the compassionate nature of his deity, the Christ, would be awaiting him on the other side of the chasm over which his own mind could not reach. To many this must seem a "cop-out" after the reasoned and dispassionate earlier approach. To others, it has the beauty of the "rebirth" of the early Christians, and is precisely as with the early Christians a personal discovery of Jesus as the Redeemer.

Obviously to Jews Kierkegaard's solution to his problem of faith is not acceptable. Neither Kierkegaard's logical mind nor ours can arrive at the answer that Jesus is the Redeemer. His "leap of faith" brought him the assurance that he sought. To some of us it seems as though the Dane scuttled all his determined program and found faith as a final magnet that irrevocably drew him to the position from which he started, safe within the bosom of his own church.

Judaism and Existentialism

To Jews the reasoning of existentialism may be interesting, though it is not at all in conformity with our tradition. Jewish tradition has always held that each of us must learn from the spiritual history of our people. We study, we learn, we interpret, we react as individuals, but the basic truths of Judaism are eternal. Each generation has a different comprehension, sets differing emphases, yet the values remain more or less constant. To deny the validity of all tradition, of the wisdom of generations of our greatest minds and hearts, and then to take a mystical leap over a precipice of not-knowing and aver that you have come home is to Judaism a strange reversal of testimony. The reaching of a personal faith in God within Judaism is the careful collecting of all evidence, of the past, of revelation, of the individual's home teaching, his school, and his own experience. Wisdom lies not in denying, but in discerning acceptance. Then no "leaps" over chasms are necessary.

A Leap from a Springboard

It is obvious that Kierkegaard's leap could scarcely have resulted in any other conclusion. We would be amazed to find this church-bred theologian leaping and ending with a devotion to Allah or Ahura-Mazda. His being a Christian predisposed him to find refuge in Christianity. So all his techniques of discovering the truth may be of interest but had little influence on the outcome of his personal search for salvation. The springboard for his leap was the catechism he learned on his mother's knee.

Is there no leap in Judaism? There may be for some of us. When study and meditation and prayer and the experience of living have joined to build a personal philosophy, we still have to accept, to depend on faith. This acceptance is, if you will, a "leap." The distance is short, but it is there.

Should man strive for perfection?

Why should man strive for perfection when he knows he won't achieve it? He knows he will sin, that despite his best intentions he will slip up some where, so if God is going to condemn him for his sins, why bother to try?

First, nowhere does it say that God will condemn him for his sins if they are all within measure and if he truly tries to repent and do better. If they are the sins of a person striving for perfection, they will probably be slight and venial, forgivable. If we do not reach toward the highest goals, we help doom the world to worse if not the worst, to evil unchallenged, to stupidity unchecked, to bigotry unconfronted.

In this sense Judaism differs from traditional Protestant Christianity which holds that man cannot do true good, that because of original sin man is so evil and addicted to sinning that only God's mercy—especially, of course, through Jesus—can possibly redeem man at all. Judaism does not agree with this concept, for we hold that man can do deeds of righteousness that have worth before God. Man is imperfect, but he can align himself with that which is good. Loyalty, trust, dedication, sacrifice, concern, these are the hallmarks of the person who is striving toward perfection, and we hold that they have value and worth, even before God.

Imitate God

We are commanded to imitate God. The rabbis asked, "How can we walk after God, whose ways are paths of fire?" They answered their own question by saying, "At the beginning of the Torah He clothes the naked (Adam and Eve), and at the end He buries the dead (Moses). So we must emulate His deeds of loving-kindness" (Sotah 14a).

No, we cannot reach perfection in doing such deeds. Our will, our comprehension are short of perfection. Yet if man is not perfectable, he is improvable. Each act of loving-kindness erases a bit of evil and brings goodness into being. The Hasidim said that through deeds of loving-kindness we restore to God that which is truly His. Slowly, we help move the world forward.

As we read in Pirke Avot, "We cannot finish the work, neither are we free to desist from it" (2:21).

What is Jewish teaching concerning women?

Even in pre-Talmudic days recognition was won by women of high talent, Deborah in Israel's heroic epoch, the prophetess Hulda in the time of the kingdom of Judah, and the reign of Queen Salome was a golden age in Jewish history.

The position of woman as mother is higher in Jewish tradition than in any other system of antiquity. The Fifth Commandment demanded that the mother be honored equally with the father. Unlike Telemachus in the first book of the Odyssey or indeed Jesus, who reproved his mother publicly, the Talmud speaks of the great reverence the rabbis showed their mothers in private and in public. Even if a mother reproves her grown son in the presence of his colleagues and his pupils, the rabbis held the son must hold his peace.

Wife and Mother

Women were not given the same duties and responsibilities as men for two reasons. The first is that they were considered too readily swayed by their emotions. We have a vestige of this today in that a wife may not testify concerning her spouse. The second is that the wife is considered to be the more important parent where the children are concerned, and therefore she is duty bound to give her energy and her time to the home and the upbringing of her sons and daughters. Because the rabbis recognized the devotion necessary for raising worthy children, they said the woman is free from any commandments which must be done by a certain time each day. So a woman may pray, but she need not—whereas a man must fulfill these obligations.

As the late Herbert Loewe of Cambridge University wrote, "Because her first duty is to her children, these have the first call on her time. Not even an angel is given two missions simultaneously" (Montefiore & Loewe, The Rabbinic Anthology, p. 656).

Although there are rabbinic remarks which do show little respect for the intellectual qualities of womankind, yet there were rabbis who responded to speak of women with the highest respect. The tractate Nidda of the Talmud, which contains some of the most damaging remarks, contains this statement from the lips of Judah the Prince, perhaps the greatest of the rabbis, "The Holy One, blessed be He, endowed woman with more understanding than man" (Nidda 45b). And we read of Beruriah, who is the spiritual and intellectual match of her husband Meir, one of the giants of rabbinic lore.

The Bringer of Blessing

The rabbis recognized the profound importance a woman has in determining the success of a marriage, the happiness of the home, and the upbringing of the children: "Whatever blessing dwells in the house, comes from the woman" (Baba Metzia 59a). "Your wife has been given to you so that with her you may fulfill life's great plan; she is not yours to vex or grieve, for if you do God notes her tears" (Ketubot 61a).

They spoke often, as did the author of the book of Proverbs, of how glorious life is with a good wife, a woman of valor (Proverbs 31). "He who has won a wise woman by his own worth has won the chief victory of life" (Zohar 3:52a).

There is often a sense of kindness and concern expressed by the rabbis. "If your wife is short, bend down to hear her whisper" (Baba Metzia 59a). "A man must love his wife as himself, and honor her more than himself" (Yevamot 62b).

At worst the rabbis did not speak of women very differently than did Paul—that women be veiled in assemblies, be silent and obey (I Corinthians 11:5, 6; 14:34). Never are rabbinic remarks on the level of those of some of the church fathers, such as Tertullian's, "The judgment of God upon your sex endures even today; and with it inevitably endures your position as criminal at the bar of justice. You are the gateway of the devil" (Women's Dress I).

The rabbis often spoke of women with genuine respect. In the Midrash we read that the rabbis were challenged to explain why Deborah was made judge and prophet although she lived at the same time as Phinehas the high priest. Their response has a universalism that includes men and women, and all humankind: "I call heaven and earth to witness, that whether it be Gentile or Jew, man or woman, manservant or maidservant, according to his deeds does God's spirit rest upon him" (Tanna debé Eliyahu 48).

How do Jews feel about miracles?

Let us first say what we understand by miracles. We are not using the word to describe an effort that seems bound to fail but succeeds because of spirit and determination, such as the victory of the Maccabees. We are not speaking of the wonders of creation, which we believe were according to plan and the laws of nature and science. We are not even using it for the wonder of existence and growth, as expressed in the siddur, "You renew each day the wonders of creation." We are not using it poetically. We are using it to describe feats or actions which seem to contravene nature. Elisha causing an ax handle to float (II Kings 6:6) is the kind of miracle we discuss here, an act not merely beyond rational understanding but actually contravening our knowledge of scientific law.

The Main Stream

Normative Judaism (the main stream of Jewish life and thought) has put no credence in miracles for a very long time. The early prophets performed miracles; the stories of Elijah and Elisha are replete with them. The later prophets reported their visions; they were not interested in physical miracles. Miracles of the spirit, yes—but they were beyond a conjurer's tricks.

There are miracles reported in the Talmud; there is little insistence on them. A miracle-worker like Honi HaMeagel puts in an affectionate appearance, but it is with an amused sidelong glance. He is not central to the thrust of rabbinic teaching, which deals with law and ethics, not miracles. A major reason why Jews did not flock after Jesus and his heralded miracles was that the people had been deceived by miracle-working thaumaturgists (faith healers) before.

Despite the usual rationalist approach of Judaism, within the constant mystical tradition that has simultaneously been part of Judaism for at least two thousand years, belief in miracles has always continued. A major reason for the fanatical defense of Jerusalem in 70 C.E. was the expectation that God would intervene miraculously between the Jews and their Roman oppressors. The men of the second Temple were good and observant Jews; The Romans were pagan and cruel. Therefore the Jews said that God had to perform miracles to rescue His holy city and His faithful ones. If Johanan ben Zakkai had not escaped from the city to establish a *yeshiva* at Yavneh, all of Judaism might have gone down to total destruction because of the fanatic belief that God had to intervene miraculously.

The weight of Jewish learning has been antimetaphysical. But the mystical tradition has persisted, manifesting itself in times of grave persecution as an escape from the horrors of reality.

Through the long centuries men of the most logical minds yet spent part of their studying hours in the mystical intricacies of Kabbala, with its teachings of constant and ongoing miracles in life. Nachmanides, the great Biblical commentator, and Joseph Karo, the great codifier of the *Shulchan Aruch*, seeming the most rational of intellects, each was a profound believer in miracles.

Hasidism and Miracles

Belief in present-day miracles persists with the Hasidic movement, which is the successor to the mystical movements of the Jewish past. Modern Hasidim insist that some of their *tzaddiks* can and do perform miracles, thought reading, thaumaturgy, even physical miracles. Not only the Baal Shem Tov, the founder of Hasidism, but many of the *rebbes* who followed him, were and are supposed to be able, by the power of their spirits and their knowledge of arcane law, to perform miracles for their followers.

Indeed, there are some *rebbes* who hold that miracles are fully within God's will for the world. Most of us would say this is contrary to our understanding of Judaism and science, but our failure to agree will not daunt a Hasid.

To quote the Lubavitcher *rebbe*:

> This world is not separate from the higher worlds but is simply another step, the last one of a long chain of worlds. Everything that influences this world comes from the higher ones. A miracle is something that happens which you could not have calculated. When a Jew connects his Divine spark with God through prayer, Torah and *mitzvot*, he can affect things in the physical world that are beyond calculation. This power is not the prerogative of one Jew but of every Jew.
>
> (A Thought for the Week, Vol. IV, No. 27)

How far can we rest on the authority of the Torah, and where must we turn to personal revelation?

In traditional Judaism the authority is in the Torah and the Talmud, or more specifically in the Shulhan Aruch, which is the code of Jewish law by which Orthodox Jews live. Yet ultimate responsibility lies in the individual. The Torah and the Talmud are books, God given, repositories of the greatest wisdom and spirit, yet books all the same. It is the individual who must react to the inspiration and the teachings and determine his role. The most Orthodox Jew is a free agent. His loyalty is to God, but his mind is his very own.

A Private Conduit

Only in Hasidism is this responsibility shared with another, or indeed given over with joy and loyalty to another, to the *rebbe* or *tzaddik*. The *rebbe* by virtue of his holiness is supposed to have a private conduit to God, and thus his followers depend on his guidance. The Hasid turns over the reins of his life to the *rebbe*, who through his intercession with God on behalf of his followers is their *rebbe*, their master. The Hasid will heed his *rebbe's* every word, for his voice is the immediate echo of divinity.

Normative Judaism, whether Orthodox, Conservative or Reform, does not lean on personal revelation. This refusal is born in the realization that personal revelation is the most difficult area for logic to police. One person's vision is theophany to him—and blasphemy to his neighbor. Visions can be bought too cheaply today. Drugs, liquor, hallucinogenic mushrooms, fasting, a high fever or madness, all produce visions even more consistently than does religious fervor. The rabbis 2000 years ago turned from personal revelation to decisions made by the congregation or by the Sanhedrin in the first democracy in religious history.

Private Criteria

Decisions were made by the people themselves, or by the rabbis meeting in open session. No longer was rule vested in a hereditary priesthood, or in a monarchy. The minority was allowed to speak, and its opinions were not only respected but were recorded, as we find in the Talmud.

There is another side to personal revelation, one more common in this age: The desire to make up one's own mind unhampered by any outside system or heritage, no matter how ancient, how authoritative.

The difficulty with this is that too often it means establishing man's most finite mind as final judge. Indeed, often it will mean establishing even the uninformed mind as judge.

Too often today men will come to decisions as to what they hold to be the vital criteria of their lives, using whatever sensibilities they possess—or misdirected by their own obtuseness, passions, or bigotry—and then turn to Scripture or tradition to choose whatever seems palatable to them and use this as a supposed divine buttress or sanction for their own ideas.

The founders of Reform and Conservative Judaism, Abraham Geiger and Zechariah Frankel alike, were intensely conscious of how dangerous this course may be. They themselves were scholars and tried to make innovations only on the basis of guides to change in the writings and actions of the greatest of rabbinic minds. Yet they were not fettered to the past. They used history's bright pages to illumine their way into the future.

Common Sense

Judaism usually is ballasted by simple common sense, not personal revelation. Not that we do not feel close to God. Our great seers are sources of spirit as well as wisdom. We guide our lives through study and reflection and hope to reach to wisdom.

Does Judaism believe in a devil?

Judaism does not believe in the kind of devil Christianity does. We do not think that Lucifer or Satan or the Devil rules over a kingdom of his own. There is no fallen angel who once challenged God and still hopes to supplant Him. Judaism refuses such an idea.

The great stream of Judaism however does have a Satan. The word *satan* means the "adversary." He is supposedly God's reminder that man sins and must be punished. Satan has no realm of his own, nor does he instigate evil, nor does he take pleasure when man sins. The book of Job has Satan deliberately persecuting Job, but the rabbis said that Job never existed and we must take the whole book as a parable.

The Devil and the Credulous

In previous centuries superstitious Jews did believe in a devil surrounded by a world of imps and evil spirits who were always eager to harm man. According to legend, God asked the angels whether He should create man or not, and some angels said no. When man was created these angels decided to persecute man. This concept is part of our legends and never was a belief of Judaism as a whole; yet multitudes lived their lives with such ideas. Maimonides and the Vilna Gaon spoke out against naiveté, but the average Jew continued to fear evil spirits and wear amulets against them. The stories of Isaac Bashevis Singer are filled with imps and demons.

The evil eye was a constant fear. One did nothing to attract the attention of the demonic forces. They were sure to swarm about those who were celebrating any happy occasion, a birthday, a wedding anniversary. Parents would not count their children or grandchildren aloud, for this would attract the evil eye. That is what *kana-hora* means, a Yiddish rendition of *kein ayin haraa*, "no evil eye!"

Living in a prescientific world, subject to every disease and woe man knew, it is not surprising that the Jews of yesteryear, exactly like their Christian or Muslim neighbors, were webbed in superstition.

Today only Jews from backward lands and the Hasidim are believers in such spirits. Most Orthodox Jews of America are no more superstitious than are Conservative or Liberal Jews.

Is there a conflict between Darwin's theory of evolution and Judaism?

No. Judaism is not locked in the story of creation in Genesis. Even Orthodox Jews accept the account as a teaching of the greatest spiritual and ethical importance, but not of scientific value. There is no aspect of Jewish theology that demands more than general acquiescence to the idea of God creating the world. There are Jewish fundamentalists, the ultra-Orthodox, but they are relatively few and outside the mainstream of Jewish thought.

The Midrash and our commentators have derived profound religious teachings from the first chapters of Genesis, but Jewish religious history begins with Abraham. It was the Christian world that was shaken by Darwin's thesis, as Christian theology supposes that Adam and Eve's sin angered God at all mankind, and thus original sin was born. This necessitated the whole drama of redemption, which is the Gospel story. In Judaism Adam's sin does not implicate all mankind, so there is no need to redeem the world from damnation. No article of Jewish theology is based on the eating of the forbidden fruit.

The question that remains is: Does gradual evolution, a process that may have taken billions of years, contradict our Jewish understanding? The answer again is no. We understand the growth of the world and the appearance and development of man as expressions of the God-process at work. Just as the coming together of ions and molecules formed the great galaxies and solar systems over the eons, so the cycle of growth of man is a product of evolutionary forces at work, which we believe is an expression of God's plan in execution.

Mind as a Tool

Man's mind is an evolutionary force. As animals and fish came into being and mutated, they developed individualized functions. But if an insect developed pincers or a rasp, it carried its tool as part of itself all the time. Monkeys learned to use a stick to reach that which their hands could not grasp. Man became the tool-maker, the tool-user. He learned to use his mind, and this placed him far ahead of the animal world even more than the skills he taught his fingers and his hands.

But man has progressed imperfectly. Great achievements in every aspect of science are coupled with irrational uses of force, born of bigotry, superstition, or just plain stupidity. The Biblical teachings of love and brotherhood are millennia old, yet they remain overlooked in the rush to progress.

We do not move ahead in a clean line, but by erratic leap and falling back. We reach the moon and are plagued by slums and drug addiction, and children who are stunted because of hunger of body and mind.

We say that evolution is growth with a goal. The way to such growth has been enunciated. Judaism demands that as God is a whole, man must learn to unite his energies and his strivings to reach for goals in keeping with his humanity.

Why can't I find the elation in my Judaism that the Hasidim have?

The Hasidim find great joy in their Judaism. Deliberately they cut themselves off from many of the usual pleasures of life in favor of a different kind of dedication. They want to be different.

A major reason for the Hasid's dressing in a kind of uniform that marks him as a Hasid is to be sure that he cannot take part in frivolities even if he is tempted. His long *kapata* or his long black jacket so sets him apart that he can't consider attending a play or a movie, or picking up a novel, let alone a prurient book. He does not own a television set and will look at one with little curiosity as he passes a shop window. What he sees there will only confirm his lack of interest in the usual fare of the TV viewer.

The Hasid is not bothered with styles or fads or costume. He avers his garb is Jewish garb, and if you try to say that it is really Polish dress of the 17th century, he will only smile and turn away. He has made it Jewish garb.

He does not care for jewelry; he wears none and owns none. Even his wife owns none besides her wedding ring. He usually doesn't wear a tie as it is ornament and not part of one's necessary clothing. He does have a fancy *kapata* and *shtreimel* (broad fur hat) for Sabbath and holiday use, but this he says is for the glory of the Sabbath and not for his own vanity.

The Hasid will not look at any woman except his wife. He loves his wife, but he refuses to lift his gaze to the eyes of any other woman lest he be tempted.

The role of the woman in Hasidism will not satisfy any "woman liberationist." There is a decided double standard. Not only does the man preempt the enthusiasm of formal prayer, he also does the singing and dancing. Only in the privacy of the home will the woman mildly join in sabbath *zemirot,* the lovely Hasidic songs. Her role is to be a good wife and mother and loyal Jewess. She derives her satisfaction from the realization that she is the guardian of the home. Her labors are long and many in keeping a kosher home. Her husband praises her in the words of "A woman of valor" (Proverbs 31) every Sabbath eve. Yet the satisfaction must be there, for few are the Hasidic girls who leave. The fact that they are married at 16 may also be a factor.

In This Is My Delight

If he doesn't enjoy many or most of the pleasures that provide other people's enjoyment, for it is obvious that he has no time for sports or gambling, then where is his pleasure? It is in his religion. The Hasid finds in prayer and study and sessions with his *rebbe* or *tzaddik* a joy that is a positive stimulation.

When the *tzaddik* holds a Sabbath public meal, his Hasidim throng about and remain standing near for hours. The rabbi may speak to his followers; he may remain silent. He may teach, he may not. But his every action as well as his words are treasured by the faithful who attend him.

Study and prayer to the Hasid are bridges to God. He sets aside hours each day for study, even though he may also spend eight or ten hours earning a living for his numerous progeny. The Talmud maintains that a man should study more hours than he spends on earning a living, but most Hasidim cannot attain this level. There are many who do not work and are sustained by their wives' labors or by philanthropy. To all of them, study is a sacred and joyous concentration. Few things please a Hasid nearly as much as does a *hiddush,* a new interpretation of a passage from the Torah or the Talmud.

A Man with His God

The supreme relationship in life is with God. The Hasid feels that his regimen is God ordained. He finds ecstasy in his mode of prayer before God. But even more homely things, from the way he puts on his clothing to his going to sleep at night, all is in consonance with the teachings of the *Shulchan Aruch* and the customs of his branch of Hasidism. It is a way of holiness.

He joins with his brothers in prayer and after the service they dance together for a few minutes. They enjoy a bit of brandy and herring, for the physical man must be fed as well. They sit about and sing. They study or they tell wonder stories of the past. They rise and dance again. The joy ascends with their singing.

At Simchat Torah, at Lag b'Omer, the Hasidim and their joy take on a fervor unmatched even in their usual devotion. Lost to all but the ecstacy of the holy day, they sing and dance as their souls mount up.

Hasidism, You and I

It would be wrong to indicate that the rest of us do not find delight in our Judaism. The deepest satisfaction must be beyond dancing or even the ecstasy of prayer. It must come from what Maimonides terms "doing truly because it is right." There should be great joy for all Jews at the Sabbath table, the Pesach *seder,* at all worship. The Hasidim do not find beauty in many things that most Jews do, in art and secular music, often not in the wonders of nature. They have different dreams, even though our goals are very much the same.

We too can find equal joy in our Judaism, but only when we give our religion the time, the energy, the consecration that the Hasid does. When you base your entire life on God, when He is more important than any other relationship, then any vocation or responsibility, then the joy will rise of itself.

Can we set absolute standards of ethics? Aren't all ethics relative?

Teachers rapidly discover that to some adolescents a refusal to set any standards of ethics is considered a sign of broadmindedness. Each person, each religion, each society has a right to set his or its own ethical standards, and no one may say them nay.

When asked, "What of the Nazis and their death camps?" some students have said (in the presence and hearing of this writer) that by our standards Hitler may have been evil, but by Nazi standards he was doing that which he thought was best for Germany, and so we have no right to condemn him.

Are there then no criteria by which men may make impartial decisions as to good or evil? No, these students say, for you may not impose your criteria on any other person. And what is more, all criteria are arbitrary.

Relativism

Relativism is the concept that every thing must be related to everything else. It says that ethical or religious standards are the products of tradition and environment. Change the tradition or environment and you get something quite different. A woman who smoked was once considered dreadful. Today smoking is frowned upon only because it causes cancer. So changing times may affect every so-called sin.

First let us differentiate between the bedrock of ethics and the changing outlook which is sometimes termed morality. Our views on smoking or short skirts may vary with the times, and though some people will refer to them as moral issues, they are not part of the permanent which we term ethics. The Ten Commandments do not deal with ephemera. They are the basis of ethics and of law.

The rabbis said that even if the Ten Commandments were not given to man, society would have to develop according to the natural law, the seven basic principles enunciated in the laws of Noah which deal with fundamental human relationships. These, the sages said, could be reached by man's mind.

Otherwise human society is so degraded that it is below the level reached by the more intelligent beasts and insects.

A Cheap Way Out

Relativism is much too easy, for it allows us to avoid the encounter with the ultimate. It allows us to hide from a sense of urgency in ethical or religious matters. Relativism allows us to refuse to accept the need to forge commitments. The individual may sink to the level of his unprincipled society, or accept the most bestial practices if they are condoned by his society, unhampered by any higher teaching. Whether it is the murder camps of Nazism or wife-swapping among some sets today, the law is that of the glorified state—or that of instant gratification—and the human level is that of barbarism.

To those who would say that wife-swapping and adultery hurt no one except—possibly—the individuals involved, let us say that the concept cheapens human emotion, debases marriage, and destroys love as the basis of true human relationships.

Let us answer the person who says we dare not condemn Nazism for it would be intolerant by pointing out that Nazism, Stalinism, Fascism were absolute in their intolerance of everything that diverged from their own totalitarianism.

Humanity and the Good

The human and the humane are related in more than language. Humanity can flourish only in the society that is humane in its principles and in its actions. Judaism says we can be broad in our sympathies for all men, and yet set standards of conduct. When evil flourishes because men are too complacent or too selfish to recognize it and do away with it, we have the basis of a new Sodom or another Nazism. Crying peace, peace, where there is no peace was not only a crime against the people in Jeremiah's day. It is as criminal now as it was then. Prophet or layman, we bear the responsibility of living by standards worthy of man—or God.

This is the challenge presented by Judaism. To fail to respond is to falter in the very concept of man. To accept it is to accept responsibility and ongoing living relationship with man and with God.

Why should we remain Jews?

This question has confronted Jews ever since the dawn of the Enlightenment in the 18th century. Earlier—and to traditional Jews, to this day—the Covenant at Sinai made the question irrelevant if not blasphemous. God had chosen His people for His divine purposes. The role of the Jew was to be accepted with fealty and joy. Once the question was allowed, once it was possible to even doubt that each Jew was a Jew because God had so willed it, the seamless link with God had developed a seam—for some Jews.

Early Liberal Judaism had to deal with this problem and did so positively. Logical reasons were adduced to supplant the theocentric. These justifications for continuing allegiance to Judaism and to Jewry retain their validity to this day.

Why We Are Faithful

(1) The religious mission of the Jews—the divine necessity to be mankind's teacher and exemplar of the truths of the Torah and the prophetic ideal in action. The Reformers believed and taught that Israel is unique as a people in that they were the first to receive the Torah. So they must by their own example teach these truths to their fellows.

(2) The inherent value of Jewish culture—to continue and to build on the treasure of Jewish ethical, spiritual and philosophic contributions. Judaism has given the world that which matches the contributions of any of the outstanding peoples, not only in our special field of religion and ethics, in which we are unparalleled. In addition, Jewish literature, the mass of Jewish folkways, the living concept of home and family, the idealism and attainment of the Jewish school and the Jewish community, the sense of involvement in man's progress, these are significant if not unique contributions which are yet alive and must be kept advancing for our own and the world's good. If Jews in any significant number would desert Judaism, all this would become museum memorabilia, and no longer a pulsating, continuing creation.

(3) The inability to achieve universalism except as mediated through a particular tradition. The person who leaves Judaism has dropped his identity and gained no other. He is despised by those he left and suspected by those he would join. Jews who throw off their Judaism have often failed to find acceptance in the outside world. They are considered by friend and enemy as Jews—and at times have brought dire consequences to their former brothers. Indeed, there are some who have become anti-Semites or foes of the state of Israel, seemingly as their own version of the price they must pay to achieve a new status.

(4) The persistence of anti-Semitism directed even at the convert. Hitler and Stalin were alike in considering anyone born of Jewish stock a Jew despite renunciation and even conversion. Hitler's minions slew nuns and priests of Jewish extraction. These unfortunates didn't even have the satisfaction of dying for *Kiddush HaShem,* the Sanctification of God's Name, as did their believing fellow victims. Karl Marx was baptized as an infant, and yet Jewry has suffered persecutions because Judaism is blamed for his teachings. He who does not add subtracts.

(5) The psychological damage which results from a denial of a conscious or unconscious element of one's identity. Jung said that when a person breaks with his religious past, he breaks with his folk ethos, his folk soul. Unless there is a clear new identification, he breaks with his own roots, the foundation of his living, and so places his psyche on shifting sands.

(6) The breaking of faith with those who lived, suffered and died for the perpetuation of the ideals of Judaism. Baptism led to easy acceptance in most ages. But our forefathers endured for what they conceived as the truth, as religion at its highest. They would not abandon a beleaguered people, especially to go over to the persecutor.

Today with the memory of the Six Million still fresh in our minds, every leaving is a desertion, a victory for Hitler.

Universalism

There are some who for the highest ideals deliberately leave Judaism and the Jewish people to embrace what they term "universalism," that all men shall be brothers on God's green earth. The experience of history demonstrates that those who dropped their Judaism to embrace the greater world, through their own naiveté lost their own contact with Judaism, weakened Judaism and Jewry, and failed to gain for themselves or for the world any real improvement. Instead they often won the scoffing of others as "deracinated cosmopolitans" or as "Godless Jews." Judaism lost doubly, for it lost the loyalties of these often brilliant individuals, and won the contumely of those who despised them. Too often it seemed as though rather than presenting an avenue to universal brotherhood, their leaving was an escape from their Jewishness and its responsibilities.

Among the world's most profound and universal teachers were the prophets. Speaking within the Jewish spectrum, they enunciated truths which embrace all mankind: "Have we not all one Father, did not one God create us all? Why therefore do we deal treacherously brother against brother?" (Malachi 2:10).

When will the Messiah come?

A question with many answers. Many Christians and Jews believe that he will come when God wills it and not before. The time of his coming is God's decision which cannot be hurried and cannot be earned. They believe that this decision to send the Messiah will be a gift of God's—which some men call "grace"—and man can only hope or pray for it, for he cannot affect its arrival or withholding.

Some individuals, Christians and Jews, have used the last chapters of the book of Daniel to try to ascertain when God intends to send the Messiah. Christians add computations from the book of Revelation. The great physicist Isaac Newton spent years at such figuring, but he was no more successful than lesser men.

The rabbis soon became opposed to such attempts. They said that God cannot be hurried, and attempts to force Him to speed the Messiah's coming are blasphemous. They said that men who spent years on calculating when God planned to send the Messiah were wasting their lives.

Elijah the Precursor

Through the ages many Jews thought that the Messiah was already on earth, waiting for the proper moment to disclose himself. He was supposedly accompanied by the prophet Elijah, who had the role of announcing his coming. So legends tell of the Messiah dwelling among humble people while Elijah helped get the world ready for the great day. Since the era of the false Messiah Sabbetai Zevi in the 17th century, such legends have lost most of their currency. They were dangerous and misleading.

To some Jews, the coming of the Messiah meant the completion of a definite period of time. To others, it was the emptying of the fount of tears, for his appearance was to be preceded by "the pangs of the Messiah," a period of grave travail. It was thought that man's sorrow would somehow earn the great day. Many Orthodox Jews thought the Nazi holocaust had to bring the Messiah, as it was mankind's greatest horror. To some, the establishment of the state of Israel was a precursor to the coming of the Messiah, the first step to redemption.

To some traditional Jews, the Messiah will only appear when all Jews observe the Sabbath in proper fashion. Many Jews and Christians as well are firmly convinced that he will come soon, very soon. Hasidic Jews and Christian "adventists," though holding exceedingly different ideas of the Messiah, agree that his coming is at hand.

45

Prepare the Way

The usual liberal Jewish way of speaking of the Messiah is that he will come when men have accomplished the necessary preparations. The predictions of the prophets must be fulfilled, that man will learn war no more and live together in peace. There must be true justice and brotherhood for all. There must be neither poverty nor oppression nor prejudice, and all will be filled with God's spirit. Only then will the world be ready for the Messiah and deserve his coming.

A major virtue of this answer is this: If no generation deserves the Messiah because all are sinful, God cannot be expected to choose one generation over the others. But if the messianic age must be prepared by man on earth, it is not God who will choose, but mankind. The generation that matures sufficiently to live by God's criteria will have ushered in the Messianic age. If one says, "Why then will we still need the Messiah?" the answer is: Man himself must be the Messiah.

One of the main purposes of the Torah and the prophets is to provide mankind with the teachings and the inspiration needed. One of the main purposes of life is for man to fulfill these teachings. That is why liberal Judaism speaks of a Messianic age, and not of the Messiah as such. It is each individual's duty to try to bring this Messianic age into being, and so every human being can become a herald of the Messianic age.

Must a Jew believe in the coming of the Messiah? Would an ideal society satisfy?

The word messiah means "the anointed one," and originally was applied to each king and high priest, for they were consecrated to carry out the purposes of God. The term was used by the prophet Isaiah to describe the Persian king Cyrus when he liberated the Jews from Babylonia (45:1). Technically speaking, every king of western Europe today is a messiah since he is anointed at his coronation. During prophetic times the term came to be identified with the divine kingship which would redeem Israel and usher in God's kingdom. Today the word is used only in that sense.

Jewish tradition holds that the Messiah will establish an age of universal peace, justice and prosperity. He will bring about the spiritual regeneration of all humanity. Even in prophetic days the messianic era was considered to hold a golden promise for all mankind (see Isaiah 65).

During the Second Commonwealth the idea was enlarged and miraculous events were supposed to accompany his advent. Not merely peace and justice, but the final judgment, the raising of the dead, the end of time, etc., were to result. Examples of this type of thinking exist in the second half of the book of Daniel, and in Esdras II of the Apocrypha. Normative Judaism refused to accept most of these apocalyptic writings into the Biblical canon. Christianity did accept many of these writings and held that they would be fulfilled at Jesus' second coming, as it was obvious that they did not eventuate in his first sojourn on earth.

The Reign of Righteousness

Judaism still posits the coming of the messiah. It will be the reign of truth and justice and peace, with the Jewish people fulfilling their role by teaching mankind God's ways. The messiah himself will be a human being, not a unique son of God or any such immortal. He will be a scion of the house of David. He will rebuild the Temple on Mount Moriah. The ultra-Orthodox aver that he will reinstitute the Temple sacrificial cult, though many of the Orthodox hold that he will—through divine inspiration—change the bloody program into something more acceptable to modern thinking. Liberal Judaism speaks of a messianic age rather than a personal messiah, the need to build a world based on the teachings of the Torah and the prophets, a world worthy of God.

Orthodox Jews confirm their belief in the coming of the Messiah at every service for their liturgy contains direct reference and promise. It is one of the principles of Maimonides' thirteen essences of faith in Judaism. Liberal Judaism does not so demand, even though it does advocate the teaching of a messianic era and asks that each Jew work for such a time.

The Coming of the Latter Days

Orthodoxy prohibits the calculation as to when the messiah will come and, even more, prohibits hastening his coming by any magical rite or by any other program except prayer (Sanhedrin 97b). The belief in the messiah, however, has been an important reason why Judaism has prevailed during the worst periods of persecution—at long last the balance will be redressed and truth and justice will triumph. The messiah will appear to establish God's reign over His people and all the nations will come to share in the ultimate redemption.

Liberal Judaism speaks of the ideal society as the only way mankind can deserve the messiah's coming. Only when men live up to the prophets' messages of peace, brotherhood and spirit will the earth be ready for the messianic age. By uniting in creating such a world mankind will have taken up the mantle of the messiah, establishing a world worthy of the God who created it. Society and each individual will reach the perfection of growth and purity inherent within themselves.

Herod was an evil man; we are not evil. Why may we not rebuild the Temple?

Herod was not a good man, and yet he rebuilt the Temple without halting the sacrifices a single day and made it more glorious than it had been for centuries. It was his own pride that led to his determination to rebuild. The Temple had been erected by Nehemiah and Zerubabel after their return from exile as an unpretentious building. Herod considered it beneath his dignity as king of the Jews. When he announced his plans the priests and rabbis were suspicious, but as soon as his men assembled the stones and other materials at the site he had no difficulty in having the old structure razed. His workmen carefully tore down only a bit of the old building at a time, and the sacrificial cult was able to go on without cessation. So Herod's new edifice was a continuation of the old rather than a reinstitution of the Temple cult.

After Herod's Temple was destroyed in the year 70 C.E., the Romans did not permit the Jews to rebuild it. They saw how holy the Temple was to the Jews and that it was a focus for their rallying together. Hadrian had every last piece of the Temple destroyed and forbade the Jews to go near the site under penalty of death.

The great retaining wall, which we call the Western or the Wailing Wall, is the only standing portion of Herod's construction. Hadrian's soldiers spared it because it was not a proper part of the Temple itself. Archeologists have recently discovered a few other mementos of the Temple, some steps, a few engraved stones, that is all.

The Dome of the Rock

Today the Islamic shrine of the Dome of the Rock stands on the site of the ancient temples. It is a structure of great beauty and historic worth. It is most sacred to the Muslims. It was built at the end of the seventh century and had been refurbished often since then. Even the thought of razing it would be considered sacrilegious by most people.

Not only Muslims but almost all Jews as well refuse to consider the rebuilding of the Temple. Orthodox Jews maintain that only the Messiah can give the signal to reinstate the Temple as the center of Jewish worship. Sacrifices have not been performed in Judaism for 1900 years. They cannot be reinstituted except by the express command of the Messiah. Only he could rehallow Mount Moriah to permit the Temple's rebuilding.

Liberal Jews too would not like to see the Temple rebuilt, but for very different reasons. The Temple housed Israel's sacrificial cult. Few modern Jews would want to see animal sacrifices restored for any reason. Many Orthodox Jews too realize that Judaism has long outgrown animal sacrifice.

So despite the fact that the present leaders of Israel are far better persons than Herod was, despite the fact that Israel has political control of the Temple Mount, there are few today who would wish to have the Temple rebuilt.

What is the meaning of blessing?

A blessing in Hebrew is a *beracha*. Every prayer that begins, "Blessed are You O Lord our God . . . " is a *beracha*. Orthodox Jews are enjoined to recite 100 *berachot* each day, on rising, washing hands, before and after eating, putting on *tallit* and *tefillin*, at every joyous or sad occasion. They recite a *beracha* when seeing any natural phenomenon, a king or a wise man.

Man blesses God for providing the occasion he is observing. It is an expression of thanks, and more. It keeps man aware of what God does for him in every aspect of life. It is the soul of man responding to the Soul of the universe.

In Judaism no person ever blesses another, not even his own child. When the father returns from the synagogue on Sabbath eve he speaks words of blessing over his children. But he does not bless them. The *kohanim,* the priests who are descendants of Aaron, recite the threefold blessing at all festivals. In Liberal Judaism the rabbi utters the same words. The father, the *kohanim* and the rabbi beseech God to do the blessing. Only He can.

When we affix a *mezuzah* to the doorpost, we ask God to bless the home. We never bless people nor do we bless things. We hope to be worthy of God's blessing.

We Bend the Knee

The word *beracha* comes from the Hebrew root *b-r-ch*. There are two Hebrew words linked to the root, both of them applicable to the meaning of blessing. The first is *berech,* knee. When man worships God in humility, he merits God's blessing. Bending the knee is a sign of humility. Translations of the *anachnu kor'im* prayer of the *alenu* or Adoration at the close of worship read, "We bow the head and bend the knee." The word *mishtachavim* means the worshiper bends and bows and presses his forehead to the ground, as Muslims *salaam* to this day.

In the days of the Temple our ancestors kneeled and prostrated themselves. In traditional synagogues on the High Holydays, when the service recounts how the high priest would prostrate himself, the cantor—and some of the most pious individuals—prostrate themselves with their foreheads on the ground. They are seeking God's forgiveness and His blessing by bending the *berech*.

An Overflowing Spring

The other form of *b-r-ch* related to *beracha* is *beraicha,* a spring of water. A *beraicha* is different from a well in that it overflows of itself, the water pouring forth to bring life to all about. One can appreciate the concept if one traverses the arid Negev or the shores of the desolate Dead Sea to come upon one of the few springs that gush from the rocks. At Ein Gedi the spring cascades into a pool and flows on. Only a few yards away the soil is rock and dust. Where the spring's waters flow they bring greening and life. Fruit and shade trees spread their branches and crops thrive. Man can flourish through the blessing of the *beraicha.*

We are reminded of the great blessings promised to the Israelites, "And all these blessings shall come upon you and overtake you, if you will listen to the voice of the Lord your God" (Deut. 28:2). The blessings seem like living things. It is as though man's deeds of goodliness give birth to more deeds of goodness, to make his life even more blessed.

It is not surprising that the ideal pastoral poem, the 23rd Psalm, is replete with word pictures of water, even to the cup—like the overflowing spring—running over.

Beracha is not static. It is not a set pattern of words. Blessing is a living, pulsating expression of faith in God, of thanks for His gifts to us—and, we trust, His response to our faithfulness.

Why do we pray to God?

Prayer is a many-faceted thing. It is born of ecstasy. "Prayer offered from the heart and for the sake of heaven ascends on high and pierces the firmament" (Baal Shem Tov). It can be sober and logical. "True worship is not a petition to God; it is a sermon to ourselves" (Emil G. Hirsch). Prayer is man reaching out to that which is beyond him.

The Hebrew word for "to pray" is *l'hitpalel,* which means "to judge yourself." When we pray we come into judgment before God, man standing before his Maker. But we must also recognize that the act of prayer implies that we must judge ourselves, as human beings, as Jews.

In Judaism praying is not as much a praying for things as it is a profound means of learning what we are, who we are, and what our role in life must be. Through prayer we learn to recognize our relationship with God, and with our fellow men.

From the beginning we have sought encouragement through prayer. The Psalms remind us of the troubles David went through, but he persevered and found strength. He became king and united his people. His prayers, the Psalms, gave him the strength to endure. Through the centuries multitudes have found courage or solace or inspiration in his prayers. We too can find strength and inspiration through prayer.

To this day the Psalms or the prayers composed by other great poets and writers of prayer stir us. They awaken within us the feelings that stirred them. If we can experience what they did, the prayers become ours as well. Many people today feel so close to the 23rd Psalm that they claim it as their own.

Prayers of Petition

Basically there are two kinds of prayer of petition, the communal and the private. Most petitionary prayers are spoken in the plural, for the entire community. In ancient days the people prayed for rain or dew for their crops. These prayers are still in the *siddur*. Jews who live in New York or London speak the words and somehow find relationship to the ancient world of Israel and to the Israel of today.

We pray for the good of mankind, for peace, for brotherhood, for knowledge, for God's rule on earth. There are prayers that wrong be set right, that the world and its inhabitants may grow in goodness. There are prayers for the coming of the messiah—or the messianic age.

We speak prayers of private petition, for health and relief from sickness, for alleviation of our woes, for sustenance. We pray that we ourselves may be changed for the better, "O Lord, guard my tongue from evil, and my lips from speaking guile."

Atonement

Prayers of contrition, that express our repentance for our sins, are collective prayers. We speak them not in the confessional to a priest as individuals, but with our fellows in the congregation. Sin is never a private affair that affects us alone. It is a matter that touches on all in the community. Even the most personal sin affects more than just ourselves. We build our moral sense best as part of the community.

This is also the reason why we say *Kaddish*, the prayer for the dead, within the congregation. With our fellow man, we are caught up in the tide of time, the tide of life and death. We join with our brothers and are sustained by their strength, and help sustain them.

We pray to thank God. The rabbis said that if we eat and drink and enjoy God's bounty and do not thank Him, are we not like robbers? If we should thank God for our food, how much more should we thank Him for our very lives, for our family, for love?

Prayer is for the weak, to help them continue. It is equally for the strong. Prayer is the assumption of responsibility, as it underlines the role we must perform in our lives.

Prayer is praise of God. *Halleluyah,* "praise the Lord." We must learn how to voice our praise. As the tongue-tied man cannot communicate fully with his fellow, so until we learn to pray to God, we cannot truly communicate with Him.

Prayer is the magnification of God in life. We seize hold of His glory and in so doing our lives take on some of His holiness, some of His greatness.

Does prayer really help?

There are many levels on which honest prayer can and does help. We speak of course of sincere prayer, not routine prayer, lip service prayer, though a person who enters a synagogue only out of convention may find himself truly praying. Nor do we speak of "coin machine" prayer—you drop in a prayer and out comes a gift. Prayer must be on a higher level.

One level would be that of joining with others in a common spiritual endeavor. We lift each other in prayer as we help each other in many ways. A Hasidic *rebbe* spoke of men singing better in chorus or lifting a weight with their fellows as similar to prayer in the community. We strengthen each other, and are strengthened in turn.

Direction

Prayer benefits those looking for direction in life. Multitudes have found guidance in prayer. Prayer can help resolve questions and enables us to find answers. Prayer gives resolution and the will to persist.

Another answer is found in the old adage, "He who rises from his prayer a better man, his prayer is answered." Prayer can make us better, more concerned human beings by its illumination. We can be inspired to work harder for whatever cause occupies us, for the betterment of the community.

Prayer can open our minds to recognize aspects of problems we would not otherwise have seen, social problems or limitations in our own lives. Prayer can provide guidelines or set criteria against which we measure our values.

And I Will Be Healed

Prayer can give strength to the sick. Any physician can tell of instances where prayer was effective, sometimes when medicine was not. And almost any clergyman can tell of instances where prayer for someone far away or unconscious has been efficacious—not only to the praying person, but to the ill. We cannot tell why prayer does seem to work at times and not at others, or why a person who could not be aware of the prayer in his behalf seems to respond. We can more readily understand why a person who is ill is aided by his own praying or by a dear one's prayer. The ill person is given resolve to fight and to renew inner sources of power.

Prayer is perhaps the only alleviating power in grave sorrow. When death or disaster strikes, man has few alternatives to prayer. He who has lost this ability has little to aid him.

Prayer and Worship

Some people distinguish between prayer and worship. Worship is communal prayer, prayer in the congregation, with a *minyan,* a quorum of ten or more—men in traditional Judaism, men and women in Reform. Worship is joining together in service of God. The Hebrew word *avoda* means service or work, precisely like the English word "service." Worship with the congregation strengthens all together. Why ten as the minimum? The Midrash points to Abraham challenging God's judgment on Sodom, and God's reply that He would save the city if there were ten good men (Gen. 18:32). The Midrash says that ten good men could save the city and its inhabitants (Tanhuma Vayera 8). They would pray together and be strengthened to remove the evil and thus save the city from destruction.

Prayer is the private aspect; worship the communal. There is prayer, of course, in communal worship. There may be private, inward seeking, in even the largest congregation. The personal quotient wed to the communal produced the greatest, most valid worship altogether.

Prayer not only reminds man of his place in the world, it reminds that he is a child of God, the possessor of a soul, and as such worthy to stand before God and man. Prayer summons to responsibility.

Isn't formal prayer sometimes hypocritical? Might it not be better to pray in the fields, or alone in one's house when so moved?

Sometimes a formal service may seem overorganized. Perhaps we get a feeling that not everyone there is there to pray to God. This is not new. The Tanna d'bé Eliyahu (an early rabbinic work) tells this tale. When the Day of Judgment comes and the wicked are condemned, the righteous will arise and say to God, "Sovereign of the Universe, when we were alive on earth, these men whom You have condemned would go to the synagogue early and say all the prayers, and now you have condemned them." And God will say, "With their lips they praised Me, but their acts did not praise Me."

Amos and Isaiah and Jeremiah years before had pointed this out. And yet the prophets and rabbis took part in formal worship as an integral part of life. They recognized that without the formality of prayer too often worship is lost entirely. Not every person can pray readily and with fervor, that to some prayer is as difficult as drawing a heavy load. There is the story of the Hasid who came to his *rebbe* to say that he was moving to a distant city, and asked how he could determine which *rebbe* there would be right for him.

His master said, "Go to each *rebbe* and tell him that you have trouble concentrating on prayer and ask his advice. If he gives you an answer, he is not a true *rebbe*."

Prayer Is Devotion

Prayer requires the utmost in concentration. It is not a leisure time activity. We must use all the power our minds possess. Lest we say that we might give up praying, for even the rabbis found it difficult, the Talmud reminds us that even the impious who join in formal prayer may find themselves lifted up.

The Hasidic master, the Besht, said, "We read in the Talmud that fastday prayers in which men who are not pious do not take part are not genuine worship (Keritot 6b). How is this explained? A wet log placed in the fireplace will not burn, but if it is put with ten dry logs, it will begin to burn and eventually burn as brightly. So the fervor of his fellows may lead even the sinner to true worship."

Brothers Joined

Judaism says that we must pray together because we strengthen one another. We pray as individuals, but we also pray as members of a community. Our prayers should move us to try to rebuild the world, our own individual worlds and that of the greater community beyond us. The formal service unites us with our brethren in a common reaching for that which is higher than any of us.

Prayer is also a learning experience, about ourselves and our relationship with God. If we pray only when the mood seizes us, we may never learn much about prayer or God. It is too important a matter to be left to impulse or to chance. It is almost as though we expected to learn to play the violin waiting for the impulse to play. For prayer can be an art.

Yet even the half-achieved prayer, even the prayer of a person who is not sure why he is in the synagogue altogether can be of worth. You never know when you may be moved to real prayer. And disuse produces atrophy.

A Hasidic *rebbe* would tell the impious, "No matter how far you may stray from Judaism, I beg of you, say the *Sh'ma* every day. It is a small request." The *rebbe* felt that as long as people retained some power to pray, ultimately they would be drawn back to God and His service.

What are a rabbi's duties?

The rabbi is first a teacher. We don't need a rabbi to conduct services as any informed Jew may do so. In traditional synagogues the rabbi usually plays no special role in the service. Nor is he especially a preacher. In traditional synagogues he may preach only a few times a year. A man called a *maggid* specialized in preaching, and would go from synagogue to synagogue, from city to city, to preach on Sabbath afternoons.

In traditional communites the rabbi serves as a judge. He sits as part of a *beit din,* a Jewish court of law, with other rabbis. In ancient days the *beit din* dealt with every aspect of law, civil and criminal as well as what we consider religious. Today a *beit din* deals mostly with matters of marriage, divorce and inheritance. The rabbi also answers and decides questions for private individuals.

The rabbi is usually the most Jewishly learned person of his community, though there are laymen who too have spent much of their lives in Jewish study. The rabbi uses his knowledge as a judge and as a teacher, and he teaches adults as well as children. Though he does not preach, he conducts a *shiur,* a discussion class, in the Talmud every Sabbath afternoon.

In Liberal synagogues the rabbi is again first a teacher. However, his sermons are a major part of his teaching. He teaches children in the religious school, adults in the adult education classes, and addresses the wider community in his sermons and lectures.

The rabbi also conducts funerals, performs weddings and other religious ceremonies, as does his traditional colleague. The rabbi directs the synagogue in that his is the main responsibility for its position in the life of its members.

Wisdom Must Rear Her Pillars

The Liberal or Conservative rabbi, like his Orthodox counterpart, must spend time in study, for Jewish knowledge—like any knowledge—must constantly be renewed and expanded.

Besides all this, the rabbi represents the Jewish community to the outside world. He take part in interfaith activities and teaches non-Jews as well.

Some people would say that the rabbi's chief duty is to the individual members of his congregation, counseling them, helping them in times of stress, visiting them when ill, easing their sorrow in hours of tragedy, offering Judaism's vision and support.

Actually, it is impossible to say which of these activities is the most important. They are all part of a rabbi's work.

What is the purpose of the Bible?

The Hebrew name of the Bible is *kitvei kodesh,* Sacred Writings, or Holy Scriptures. The Hebrew name is in the plural because the Bible is actually thirty-nine books and not one. It is a library in one thick volume. This plurality emphasizes how difficult it is to frame one answer to cover the question, for it might be rephrased: What is the purpose of each of the thirty-nine books of the Bible?

There are books of religious poetry (Psalms), of history (Judges, Kings), of wisdom literature (Proverbs, Ecclesiastes), of pastoral narrative (Ruth), and books which are a compound of all of these (the Five Books of Moses). We are presented with the sweep of Jewish history, with the quiet wisdom of Proverbs, with the intense seering message of the prophets.

The Knowledge of the Holy Is Understanding

The rabbis always held that our Scriptures are didactic, that they were meant to teach. They labored long to interpret the text to derive the utmost of religious, ethical and spiritual instruction, as well as *halachah,* Jewish law. Some rabbis maintained that every line has a mystical meaning to be comprehended only by the initiate. The traditional Jew holds that every letter of the Bible is holy and contains meaning for mankind. Even such sections that may seem outmoded to us provide them with material for instruction. So, for instance, the section on leprosy in Leviticus became the basis for a lesson on slander which is pertinent to us all today.

Our Bible's major purpose is to be mankind's prime teaching of religion, of faith in God, of the way God acts in our world, of what He demands of man. It is divine guidance leading to a holy and fruitful life. It warns against evil and sin. It directs man to act righteously and spiritually. It provides spiritual groundwork for ethical thought and action. It comforts those in trouble, provides guidance for those in need. It scourges the complacent. It is a living force, the spirit of man captured in a book which you can hold in your hand and in your mind.

Professor Abraham J. Heschel said that the greatest miracle of the Bible is the miracle it worked on the people who read it, studied it, and lived by it.

Did the prophets really talk to God?

They firmly believed they did. And they spoke in His name. The word *nevi-im* in Hebrew really means "forthsayers," or "spokesmen for God," as someone put it. Foretelling the future was not their role, so the word "prophets" was ill-chosen to depict them. They spoke God's message to the people. The people did not always hearken. Some of the prophets suffered because of their temerity, for they arraigned kings and priests, nobles and the wealthy. Some were jailed. Amos probably was killed. They persisted because they had to fulfill their missions.

We have no way of proving that it was God's message they spoke except from the evidence of their writings and the effect on society for millennia. Nowhere in all of world history or world literature is there a large group of men who produced such an exalted body of teaching and religious poetry as did our prophets. In a tiny country, over a period of a thousand years, one after another they arose, men and women, to inspire and to instruct mankind in God's ways.

If there were a few or even a dozen, we might say that this was a flowering of genius, be grateful and let it go. But there were a score and more almost unmatched in all of the world. Other lands were blessed with a Zoroaster, a Buddha, a Lao-tze or Confucius. Tiny Israel produced Moses and Deborah, the two Isaiahs, Jeremiah, Amos, Micah, and the others.

Their messages were delivered to the Israel of the time; much of their prophecies was meant for all mankind through the ages. Transcending time and place, the prophets' messages laid the groundwork for the world's teachings of religion, spirit, and ethics. Few men in the more than 2000 years since their day can begin to match their incredible achievements. If this was not God's inspiration, no other explanation will begin to do.

Some religious thinkers believe that somehow man was closer to God in those days. The simplicity of man's existence did not set up barriers between him and God. They say that the prophets understood divinity more clearly than men of any other era. So we study and cherish their words.

The Bible teaches, "Eye for eye, tooth for tooth." Isn't this proof that Judaism is a religion of vengeance?

Rather than being proof of a lust for revenge, the Biblical text (Ex. 21: 24) and the rabbinic discussions and decisions based on it are vivid statements of Judaism's recognizing how primitive was blood vengeance and replacing it with a system as modern as our workmen's compensation laws.

Most of the peoples among whom the Israelites dwelled lived according to the code of vengeance. If anyone was injured, whether willfully or accidentally, he took physical vengeance. The avenger sought no measure for measure, eye for eye, tooth for tooth. The revenge was death.

If a person was killed, even accidentally, the whole family or clan was obligated by custom to take vengeance—not only on the perpetrator of the death, but on his whole family or clan. And after their own first death, the opposite family or clan was obligated to seek revenge in turn. The duty to slay fell on every male, their victims would be any member of the offending group, women and children, the lame, it made no difference. Every successful killing, even of a child, was greeted with celebration.

This code of honor persists to this day among the Bedouins and some other Arabs. A series of formal transactions are necessary to end such a feud, which otherwise can persist for decades. The Israeli police go to great trouble to stop such feuds.

The Talmudic Understanding

In earlier years there was no authority which could try to end these blood feuds which would take innocent lives and embitter a whole region.

The "eye for eye" text prohibited just this sort of vengeance and so obviated the blood feud. The Talmud shows how the Jews even in ancient times interpreted this passage. It was regarded as formulating laws for the payment of monetary damages for injuries suffered. The priests and judges had indicators. They pointed out that the Torah says, "Who kills an animal shall pay for it, life for life" (Lev. 24:18). As no Jewish court would condemn a man to death for slaying a beast (in contrast to English courts until the 19th century), hence the Talmud said that such expressions signify payment.

Lest anyone cavil and say that this is a much later rabbinic softening of the original laws of taliation, let us refer to the Akkadian code of King Eshunna, of the Babylonian kingdom, 20th to 19th centuries B.C.E., which antedates the laws of Hammurabi by at least 150 years. Gouging out an eye cost one pound of silver, but breaking another man's tooth was cheaper.

From all evidence this was the way the Israelites handled the matter, even in earliest days. The rabbis were more flexible in that each injury was judged according to well-established sets of value which took into consideration the extent of the injury, medical costs, the pain suffered, time lost from work, payment of others to do the work of the injured person—which is precisely the way present workmen's compensation laws operate (see the Talmud, Baba Kamma 83b, for the entire discussion). This is not vengeance; it is justice at its fairest.

Do we have to believe in the miracles of the Bible?

There are two categories of miracles: those which seem to be just legends (those of Elijah and Elisha); and those which seem central to our understanding of Judaism (the crossing of the Sea of Reeds, the plagues in Egypt, the manna). The first demands little attention as these miracles are peripheral to any understanding of Judaism. The miracles of Elijah and Elisha seem to be folk memories of a more credulous age. The Jews rapidly outgrew dependence on miracles so that the later prophets never depend on magic to impress the populace. The gravity of their message was far more compelling than any miracle.

The second category demands attention. These Biblical recountings are too important merely to say they are folk legends interwoven in the fabric of our history, though this is what many scholars maintain, and this explanation may be satisfying. Most Jewish scholars maintain that these events were natural phenomena, and their only miracle was their occurring at precisely the right time. The plagues were all natural. Even the darkness was probably an eclipse.

Though some of the Jewish philosophers held that the truth of Scriptures was demonstrated by the miracles (Judah HaLevi), the greatest of them all, Maimonides, did not. "He who comes to believe by reason of miracles retains in his heart some suspicion that perhaps these miracles were performed by magic or sorcery" (Mishne Torah, Yesode HaTorah I,8).

Both HaLevi and Maimonides thought the proof of the Torah was adduced from Sinaitic revelation and by its intrinsic excellence, that it had been proved over the centuries as the finest of all religious teachings. To our ancestors, God's revelation of the Torah at Sinai was proof—for were there not thousands present who would have contradicted the Torah account had it not been entirely true?

The modern Jew will probably agree with the philosophers that the miracles of the Bible are unnecessary to establish its importance. Even the usually credulous HaLevi finds the final proof in the Torah's exalted teachings, "the well-being of the soul and the well-being of the body" (Cuzari I, 43). This was for Baruch Spinoza the only test man could depend on (Epistolae 73:IV, 307, 15-17).

Didn't the ancient Hebrews really have a primitive idea of God?

When the Hebrews entered the land under Joshua their civilization was primitive in almost every way—except one. They were recently freed slaves, but they had the memory of ancestors who were proud, free men. The Hebrews were still in the late Bronze Age, but they possessed one thing that no other people of their time had, the vision of a single, unseen God who demanded ethical conduct and spiritual service.

Scholars do not agree as to how much of the Torah they brought with them. They had the Ten Commandments, they had the immediate memory of covenanting with God, for the Decalog is the symbol of the Covenant. They had the promise that if they obeyed the commandments, the Lord would be their God. Centuries of life would refine and develop their concept of God and His service, but the fundamental ideas were there.

Did they still consider the gods of other nations valid even though inferior to their own God? Very likely many of them did. Did some Hebrews run after these gods and give the Lord only lip service? Unquestionably many did. But with the centuries the idea of God as the sole and supreme Creator and Ruler became manifest. The prophets made plain what the priests had never been able to do.

There are remnants of ancient mythologies in our Scriptures, but they are like fossilized flies in amber, without life and transmuted in the new substance. Only by diligent peering can they be found.

The Living God

"The Lord is the true God; He is the living God and the everlasting King" (Jeremiah 10:10). This is the word of a prophet who lived 2600 years ago. This truth seemed so obvious to the early Jews that there is no theogony in Judaism, no attempt to discuss whence God arose or what were His beginnings. All ancient nations devoted much of their mythologies to this, but to the Jews God has ever been eternal. As He was Creator of all, He predates the inception of time and is not subject to it.

The ancient Jews spoke of God anthropomorphically, almost as though He was a kind of superman. It was not necessarily a primitive way of considering Him. It was a concretized poetic rendition that often accompanied a high spiritual theology.

The medieval philosophers took great pains to explain away every anthropomorphism, but the earlier rabbis were not troubled by them. They said that Scripture is God's , but it speaks in the language of man, and so considered verbal depictions of God almost as man to be the Bible's way of making God real to humans.

That God is God and not man is underlined in many ways. There is no female deity in Judaism, nor is there a son or daughter or mother of God. These are all foreign to Judaism's comprehension of God. God is beyond sex or children. We speak of all mankind as children of God, but this too is in the spiritual or poetic sense.

In addition, the commandments prohibit any making of a representation of God, so that even as superb a masterpiece as that of Michelangelo in the Sistine Chapel is blasphemy. To reduce God to human level was inconceivable. "I am God and not man" (Hosea 11:9).

The One God

From Biblical times the people of Israel have averred that God is the one and only true God. Professor W. F. Albright said that we can speak of monotheism from the age of Moses, "of only one God, creator of everything, the source of justice, who is powerful in Egypt, in the deserts and in Palestine, who has no sexuality and no mythology . . . cannot be seen by human eye and cannot be represented in any form" (From the Stone Age to Christianity, p. 207).

Certainly within a few years after the establishment of the Jewish kingdom, the prophets were affirming the universality of God (Amos 3:2; 9:7).

61

The deities are blocks of wood or iron. They are only to be scoffed at [Elijah and the priests of Baal (I Kings 18)]. The Lord dominates all creation and all history; there is no room for any other deity. God's rule is one of spirit and ethics, of the highest in duty to one's brother and to Him. God's concern for man is born out of His love. History will find its true meaning only when all the peoples willingly come to the worship of the Lord.

Deutero-Isaiah lived 2500 years ago. Few if any are the significant advances in religious creativity since his death. All great religious thought since then has been but commentary. Go and learn!

Is there anything wrong in using the expressions "Old Testament" or "A.D.?"

In considering the Bible we must distinguish between the Hebrew Scriptures and the Old Testament. The Old Testament is a way of reading Hebrew Scriptures in the light of Christian revelation and theology. It presupposes that the New Testament fulfills the predictions and promises of the Old Testament, and so supplants it. The Hebrew Scriptures are in no way incomplete. The use of the term "Old Testament" links our Bible with a "New Testament" and grants the latter work at least equal validity, which it does not have according to our understanding. Also, we are conditioned to think that the new anything, whether the latest motorcar or fashion, makes the old obsolete.

The founders of Christianity who coined these terms were signifying that the prophecies of the Old Testament were incomplete, that the Gospel stories were needed to complete the work, that their Scriptures superseded the old. They used the Hebrew Bible as a mine, drawing out that which they considered essential to their own faith. Its importance to them was that it could be useful to bulwark Christianity. It had little importance in its own right.

So, for instance, the great teaching, "You shall love your neighbor as yourself," is presented by Christians as a major contribution of Jesus. Yet it is first enuciated a thousand years before in the Hebrew Bible (Lev. 19:18).

Once we understand this, we can appreciate why we should always refer to our holy writings as the Holy Scriptures or Hebrew Bible—and never as the Old Testament.

Anno Domini

So too the Latin term *anno domini,* which is A. D. spelled out, is an irrelevant one for Jews. The words mean "in the year of our Lord," and refer to Jesus. As in the "Lord's Prayer," the word "Lord" is Jesus and not God, and underlines the basic difference between Judaism and Christianity.

The Jewish terms for the secular year—we must refer to it as the secular year for not only Jews but non-Christian lands such as the Arab states and the far eastern countries use the reference date to be in accord with the lands of Europe and America—are B.C.E. and C.E., "Before the Common Era" and the "Common Era." We do not consider their use as denigrating to anyone. They express the fact.

How can I relate to the Bible?

Perhaps this question should be rephrased to read: How should an intelligent, interested person go about reading the Bible seriously? The Bible was never meant just to be read. No one can just pick it up and immediately find delight and encouragement and wisdom. The Bible is a work of delight, encouragement and wisdom, but these goals can be reached only by diligent study.

On a different level, no one tries to read Shakespeare or Sophocles without expecting to investigate commentary and footnote, so that archaisms and philosophy born of the era will become clear. How then can we come to the greatest work of all time, expecting to read it as we might a current novel? Even the most accessible portions, such as the narratives of Genesis or the Psalms, yield their richness only when they are read with rabbinic commentary.

Old and New Guides

No rabbi, even after years of intimate knowledge, will read the Bible without the great commentaries of Rashi, ibn Ezra, Abravanel, etc., at his side. There are commentaries in English written for the modern man, such as the Soncino or the Anchor series or the Hertz Pentateuch, which present much of the light of the past in convenient language. But they too require our patience.

The Hebrew Scriptures are not an easily ingested collection of books. Written over a period of a thousand years by dozens of minds, they include much of the world's greatest poetry, philosophic writing, and inspiration. Even when the text seems clear to us, we would do well to seek commentary, for ofttimes the clear surface hovers over a wealth of hidden meanings. The rabbis said that every verse of the Bible has four possible meanings: the obvious, the homiletic, that which can be reached only by careful reason and —last—the mystic.

So too only the careful searching of the past can take even the simple narratives of Genesis and show how replete they are with teachings of the deepest ethics and the highest spirituality.

The thrust of the prophets seems pertinent and available to us, but a thorough reading of Isaiah will soon show us that the book is actually many books, spoken by at least two and perhaps three Isaiahs. If you read Isaiah and at first find yourself thrilled and then find yourself lost, it is not your fault. For those seeking the passages which transcend time, it is best to use an anthology of prophetic writings which is straightforward, which does not impose a false unity, which graphically presents what the prophet in his genius truly meant on many levels.

The Translation Is a Traitor

We should of course read the Bible in the original with the commentaries in Hebrew as well. Most of us will have to be satisfied with a modern Jewish translation, though even the best translation cannot be entirely true. Anyone who insists on trying to plow his way through the King James translation is seeking majesty at the expense of intelligibility and accuracy. It is often far off course.

Remember that the Bible is a library, not a single book. Its parts vary from the weight of Job, the passion of the Song of Songs, the spiritual insights of the prophets, to the relatively lightweight Proverbs. There are also old legalisms, episodes of history dealing with ancient wars, details of sacrifice. We read them for their record of Jewish history and evolution.

Bible study is for any person who is concerned with the quality of his religious life. The Bible is the supreme source of religious wisdom, poetry and spirit. Each of us could spend his years in its study, and the wealth of commentary and midrash (amplifying stories and comments). There is no exhausting this enormous reservoir, the overflowing fountain that is the source of our ethics and spirit and our outreach toward divinity.

"Turn it, turn it," the rabbis said, "for all is within it" (Pirke Avot 5:25).

Why does God speak of the Jews as special?

We might rebut the question by asking, "Does He?" Each people should think that God's love is sufficient for all nations. Each people should feel that it has an important task in life beyond mere survival.

The Torah does speak of God setting the Jews a special purpose, to be a "kingdom of priests and a holy people" (Ex. 19:6). They are to be to Him an *am segula,* a "people set apart." They are to teach God's holiness and his moral law to mankind. For this purpose they received the Torah and from it learned how to choose between good and evil. A wise English-Jewish writer named Israel Zangwill wrote that even more than God choosing the Jews, the Jews chose God. They wanted to be on His side, to live by his teachings.

Our prayerbooks as well as the Torah speak of God "who has chosen us from among all peoples and given us His Torah." The rabbis said that God offered the Torah to many people, but they refused to accept it, as they did not want to live by its teachings (Sifri, Numb. § 89; Yoma 76a). The Israelites at Sinai responded, "All that the Lord has spoken we will do" (Ex. 19:8).

Holiness as a Path

Holiness in Judaism is not a matter of tabu or of ritual nearly as much as it is the assumption of a meritorious role in life. Our ancestors understood this as a distinct obligation. God trusted in us; we must fulfill our role. God used the Jewish people to present His teachings to mankind. Above all, we were constrained to live so as to set an example for all.

To the Jews the idea of *am segula,* even though it is sometimes translated as a "chosen people," does not mean that we consider ourselves a master race. We were not chosen to boss the world. Indeed, we were told that we were selected just because we were relatively few and powerless (Deut. 7:7).

The Role of a People

Our role is to live and to teach God's way, the way of brotherhood and peace. If we fail to do this we are unfaithful to the very idea of being a Jew. When we live up to these teachings, we are establishing God's rule in the world, making of our own lives something special.

There are Jews today who find the concept of chosenness difficult to accept, notably the Reconstructionist movement founded by Rabbi Mordecai M. Kaplan. They have changed their prayerbook to read, "who has drawn us near to His service and given us His Torah." Actually, it is a matter of words and not of role in life or even of intent. The Reconstructionists are as dedicated to the Jews' role in religion and life as embodied in the teachings of the Torah as any branch of Judaism.

To the Jews this role has been a holy charge, born of God's wish to bring His holiness to all mankind, that we may exemplify what is highest in man for all mankind.

What is a Jew?

The present state of Israel has been plagued by this question almost since it began. The legal answer has more or less followed *halacha,* religious law: a Jew is a person born to a Jewish mother, or who has been converted to Judaism according to traditional ritual—with circumcision for males, and *t'vila,* immersion in a *mikveh,* a ritual bath, for both men and women. The Israeli Supreme Court did rule that the children of a nonpracticing woman of Christian parentage and a Jewish father, both long resident in Israel, should be registered as Jewish nationals. But the rabbinate in Israel has refused to honor this designation.

The Ministry of Immigrant Absorption further complicated the matter by declaring that Israel would recognize both Conservative and Reform conversion to Judaism as sufficient to qualify a person for *aliya,* immigration, to Israel as a Jew. The Orthodox rabbinate's response was again to refuse to recognize such conversions. To the Orthodox such a person might become an Israeli national, but would still be considered a non-Jew, like the Christian and Muslim Israelis of the land. For these persons to be married or buried as a Jew, the rabbinate demands traditional conversion.

Who Is a Jew?

This would seem to presume that the standards of determining who is a Jew are religious. Yet there are well-known Jews who are not religious at all, Freud and Einstein in the recent past, Ben Gurion and Dayan today. Are these nonpracticing men still to be considered Jews?

A person may enter the Jewish community only by the formality of conversion. He leaves it the same way, the formal step of conversion to another faith. Some individuals may break away from Judaism and Jewry by attrition, by deliberately forsaking the Jewish community and losing identity as a Jew, until they are no longer considered Jews—except by a Hitler who condemned priests and nuns to the death camps because they were of Jewish descent.

The rabbis and the Jewish people have refused to consider those who opted out by joining another religion as Jews. A person who joined a Christian church or a Buddhist group is not considered a Jew any longer by the state of Israel, or by his fellow Jews. He may return to Judaism and be accepted once more as a Jew, but this requires a definite return.

During periods of intense persecution, some Jews accepted conversion to another faith to escape the sword or the pyre. There were Muslim as well as Christian Marannos, converts in name only. When they managed to escape and come back to the Jewish fold, they have always been accepted as Jews with no stigma.

But what of the positive Jew? What is a Jew aside from the factor of a Jewish mother? We do not question any Jew who is a part of the Jewish religion. Not even the most Orthodox will deny that a Reform or a Conservative Jew is a Jew. He considers them bad Jews, but Jews nonetheless. The same logic applies to Einstein and Dayan.

Judaism is more than a religion. Mordecai M. Kaplan termed it a "civilization," for it has all the ramifications of one. Judaism embraces religion, peoplehood, a land, a culture, a number of languages (Hebrew, Yiddish, Ladino), philosophy, literature. The richness of religious heritage and history link Jew to Jew in a bond that most Jews honor as themselves.

Being a Jew is a natural act that implies belonging, a fusion with a heritage that is even more than a history. It is a sense of being.

Why is Jewish family life often admired?

The Jewish family has been considered by sociologists and other concerned experts to be a more tightly knit unit than most other groups. This is not to say that all Jewish families are models of excellence, but the usual level is quite high. By all usual criteria—incidence of divorce or separation, desertion by parent or child, reports of cruelty, abandonment, drunkenness— or by positive report, the Jewish family through the ages has earned consistently high grades.

There is real relationship between parent and child, an interflow of thought, affection and care, a feeling of warmth and concern. At times the concern may seem excessive, but psychologists agree that overconcern is far better for most children than underconcern. It provides the protective nurturing ground for the young that they need, and if they flounder a bit when they leave, yet they are stronger and better equipped for the struggles of life than those who emerge from a colder, less hospitable family group.

The Religious Home

There are substantial reasons why the Jewish home is usually a good one. One is religious. Many Jewish ceremonies and observances are in the home, the Sabbath candles and Kiddush, the parental blessing. The excitement and joy of Pesach and Sukkot are in the home rather than the synagogue. The rabbis said the home became a *mikdash m'at,* a small sanctuary, when the parents create within it the warm and ennobling atmosphere of Jewish observance. The children learn that their religion, their tradition, their history are all integral parts of their lives. All interweave to produce a cloth of strength and endurance—and beauty.

This intermingling of love and religion has been a fundamental basis for the perduring of Judaism and the Jews. The converse is also true. Sigmund Freud said that he never met a Jew who had converted who did not hate his father. His reasoning was that the father image and God image became one in the person's mind, in hating the one he rejected the other. Happily, such hatred and rejection are rare. The overwhelming response has been loving devotion to parent and to God.

Refuge from the World Outside

Another reason for the good Jewish home is that the family was the haven when the Jew lived as a persecuted minority. He found his joy of existence in his religion and his family. The two were inseparable. Unlike the men in many lands, the Jewish father did not spend his leisure time in the club or cafe. He spent it in the synagogue in study or prayer—or at home with his family.

A third and compelling reason is that there was a real relationship between parent and child. The father was head of the household, yet many decisions were discussed openly. The children were encouraged to bring their problems to their parents. There might be emotional scenes, but they were expressions of deep concern, not of rejection. The child usually found help and support in almost any eventuality.

Much of these strengths of the Jewish home has continued. Any parent who reduces these strengths, robs himself and his family. Parents who let relationships slide, or expect gifts or money to make up for lack of communication, children who refuse to recognize their parents' abiding interest in their lives, are harming themselves and their family.

Whence Does My Help Come?

A recent survey asked young people to whom they would turn to help with their problems. Teachers, clergy, and most of all, to friends of their own age, they answered, but rarely to parents. This is cause for sorrow. It means they were avoiding the major source of concern and help in their need. The reasons given, "My parents wouldn't understand," "They will get too excited," or "My parents have their own lives to lead, and it would be unfair to push my problems on them"—these are unreal. If the parents and children have managed to build a solid relationship, the parents would be the natural and best aid in any circumstance.

Today in a rapidly changing society where all institutions are threatened, where mobility has often replaced stability, the Jewish family may have lost much of its cohesiveness.

The building of a fine family life, based on love, mutual concern and respect, and the Jewish teachings of ethics and spirit, becomes an even more pressing challenge. As its result will determine whether our own lives are meaningful and happy, each of us must be consecrated to do so.

Why has there been prejudice against the Jews?

Prejudice is irrational thought, born of ignorance, of emotionalism, of deliberate false propaganda. The reasons for anti-Semitism are numerous and they partake of each of these basic affronts to reason and fair play.

To accuse the Christian Gospels of prejudice seems insulting, yet every liberal theologian and church historian agrees that at times the Gospels are deliberately anti-Jewish. The Gospel of John mentions the Jews dozens of times and each time pejoratively. The four Gospels are the official stories of Jesus in the Christian Bible. They were written decades after Jesus' death. They deliberately put the blame for Jesus' crucifixion on all Jews, not on a small group of Saducees and government and Temple officials, which is the most any fair-minded historian might do. The Gospels do not blame the Romans, who were the conquerors of the land and who incontrovertably were the condemning and executing power. Instead, the Gospels excuse even Pontius Pilate, the Roman governor, though he had earned his reputation as a bloody-minded tyrant. In the Coptic Church he has been sanctified as St. Pontius, he the man who condemned Jesus to death!

The Gospels blame the Jews, and not only those of Jerusalem, who might be implicated in any plausible way. The Gospels blame every Jew in the world—and those unborn as well. The New Testament has the mob of Jews who supposedly thronged Pilate's court not only scream for Jesus' death, but also cry out that the responsibility should be on the head of every Jew, born or unborn (Matt. 27:25). So a Jewish baby born a thousand years later and a thousand miles away was considered equally guilty as a killer of Christ. Not until Vatican II of 1965 did the Roman Catholic Church officially change its teachings and state that the Jewish people as a whole could not be held guilty of the death of Jesus. But through the many centuries until then this was official church policy, taught and preached from the pulpit.

The Stranger Is an Enemy

Another major reason for prejudice is that the Jews have always been a minority. They were driven into exile and had to live by the tolerance of those about them. This tolerance was easily poisoned by theological bigotry, or by nationalistic suspicion. The Jews were different in religion and in culture. They spoke other languages, they had relationships with their brothers in other lands. So they were suspect. They were defenseless and so easy to blame. Whenever wars erupted, or there were disputes, the Jews were blamed on both sides. When the Crusaders marched against the Arabs in the 12th century, they slaughtered hundreds of thousands of Jews on their way to the Holy Land. When a natural calamity occurred, earthquake, plague, or famine, the superstitious ages blamed it on the Jews. The Black Death in the 14th century triggered dreadful anti-Semitic riots and wholesale massacres. Because the Jew was different he was forced to live in ghettos, walled in, supposedly for his own protection.

During the past 200 years, nationalism in Europe made every country feel that it had to protect its culture, its traditions, from outside influence. The fact that the Jews in every land had contributed to the well-being and to the general culture, that they had lived in the land for many centuries, these facts only made the anti-Semites angrier. They didn't want contribution; they wanted "purity." Irrational? Of course, but any anti-Semitic work shows irrationality at a fantastic level.

Down with God!

Maurice Samuel, the author, suggested that anti-Semitism is actually a form of rebellion against God. People who hate the ethical teaching of the Bible, whether in Jewish or Christian form, cannot rebel against God or the church. Neither their consciences nor the public will allow such rebellion. But by attacking the Jews they attack the people who are the source of the Bible and the church. The Roman Catholic theologian, Father Edward Flannery, in his book, "The Anguish of the Jews," spells out this idea in detail.

Anti-Semitism was also a convenient tool for politicians, to make the Jews the scapegoat, the butt of every blame. They blamed the Jew for every wrong of society, whether it could be their fault or not. This is sometimes, alas, good politics.

Lastly, anti-Semitism, like any bigotry, makes the bigot feel superior to one he laughs at—or kills. Prejudice is born in ignorance and bred in those with an inferiority complex. Prejudice is not only anti-Semitic, it is anti-religious, anti-human, and finally, anti-God.

Are Jews pacifists?

Judaism gave the world the dream of world peace as its highest goal in the celebrated enunciations of Micah and Isaiah, "And they shall beat their swords into plowshares . . . " Peace based on justice and understanding was the goal, not the Roman imposed peace, which consisted of destroying every person or movement that refused to conform.

The Jew was not warlike for eighteen hundred years. Today the state of Israel has rediscovered the military potential of the Jew. Today as in the time of Judah the Maccabee or Bar Kochba, arms are the answer to aggression, the threat of annihilation, or the destruction of the Jewish faith. But the Jew never considered war a good in itself, whether the warrior was Abner or Moshe Dayan.

The ancient Jews were renowned warriors. Mighty Rome had to bring legions from as far as Britain to overcome the defenders of Jerusalem. The Jews fought only to defend their homeland and for the right to practice Judaism freely. The Hasmonean kings did fight some wars of aggression. This is part of the reason why the rabbis condemned them.

Soldiers No Longer

The Jews who lived in the diaspora (outside the land of Israel) had little military tradition. There is a midrash, an old legend, which underlines this. It says that after the Bar Kochba rebellion, which was put down with infinite cruelty, the Jews were forbidden by the rabbis to use force to return to the land of Israel. Instead they were told to wait for the Messiah who will redeem not only them but all mankind. But the Talmud also reminds Jews that when the gentile world persecutes them too severely, when they are threatened with destruction, then they should again take up weapons (Shir HaShirim Rabba 2:18; K'tubot 111a).

According to this tradition, Hitler nullified the rabbis' pronouncement by trying to exterminate the entire people. So it was necessary for the Jew again to fight as a Jew, not just as a citizen of the country in which he made his home and to which he had sworn his fealty.

There are individual Jews who are pacifists. There are some Jews who refused to fight against Hitler, even though their refusal not only meant their own deaths but also indirectly contributed to Hitler's strength. But basically Judaism is not a pacifistic religion. The concept of "turning one's cheek" to the smiter is not a Jewish idea. Pacifism is noble in its renunciation of all violence, but it permits the rule of evil.

Judaism holds peace, just peace, as mankind's goal, but recognizes that evil and the evil-doer must be confronted. The man who is a pacifist in a world of Hitlers and Stalins either turns the world over to them, or allows his own well-being to rest on those who are willing to bear the burden of combating evil.

Holding peace as his highest ideal, yet does the Jew demand that we fight evil—and if need be, the perpetrator of evil.

Why did Hitler kill the Jews?

Germany had been an anti-Semitic country for many centuries, which made it a fertile ground for Hitler's desire that the German people hate the Jews. During the Crusades a hundred thousand Jews were slain in the Rhineland. Martin Luther, the founder of the Lutheran Church, first tried to be nice to the Jews so that he might convert them. When they remained steadfast, he became angry and his writings are filled with calumnies against the Jews and Judaism.

So the Germans were prepared to accept Hitler's accusations. Hitler may have been a failure at every thing he tried but he was a master politician. He knew the German people and how they would react. Banking on the Germans' centuries of hatred, he blamed all of the country's woes on the Jews. The great majority of Germans and Austrians accept every one of his baseless accusations. In the Jew he had the perfect scapegoat.

Weimar Germany

Germany was in a terrible depression. It had been beaten in World War I and forced by the victorious allies to pay huge reparations which broke the economic back of the country. The people's pride in their emperor, their army, their institutions, all were destroyed. Rather than blame these things on the Germans themselves, on Kaiser Wilhelm for leading them into five years of grinding war, on the bankers and industrialists who hoped to gain by German imperialism, on the general staff for their overweening ambitions, Hitler said that the Jews had "stabbed Germany in the back" because they were part of an international Jewish plot to take over the world.

Hitler said that though the Germans were "the master race," Germany was threatened by "the mongrel Jews." Only by extirpating the Jews could Germany be saved. Hitler said that the Germans were wonderful that all the great contributions to mankind were made by Germans or Germanic people. And, he concluded, they deserved to rule the world, and all they had to do was get rid of the Jews. A few good Germans protested and they were locked in concentration camps or forced to flee for their lives.

As the war went on and Hitler saw that he would lose, his hatred of the Jews increased. He would not admit that he was being defeated by British tenacity, or the rolling Russian tanks, or the overwhelming air armadas of the U.S.A. He blamed it all on the Jews. Madness drove him and his fanatic followers to try to destroy all of Europe's remaining Jews in the "Final Solution," and his victims died by the millions as Germany went down in flames.

How did God save the Jews?

In the book of Exodus we read of God saving the Jews from being slaves. This saving we call "redeeming." Without God and His inspiration our earliest ancestors would have continued as slaves and would have become absorbed and lost among the Egyptians. There would be no Jewish people, and so we say that God saved or redeemed the Jews.

Many times since God—or faith in Him—saved us. During the Babylonian exile the Jews might have been lost among their captors, as were all other ancient peoples who were sent into captivity. The Jews kept their faith in God because of His prophets, Ezekiel and the second Isaiah, who spoke in His name of Israel's future as a united people in their own restored land. The prophets and the priests taught that the practices of Judaism, its rituals and its prayers, would hold the people together until they could return and rebuild their homeland. So through faith in God the Jews were redeemed.

In the time of the Maccabees only their devotion to God kept the Jews alive before the might of the Syrian Greeks. All other peoples under the rule of the Syrian Greeks abandoned their own religions and ways and accepted the Hellenic pagan gods. Faith and perseverance kept Judaism and the Jews alive.

The Threefold Bases of Judaism

When the Temple was destroyed by the Romans, the rabbis kept the people and Judaism alive only through their deep faith in God. They said that prayer, study and deeds of loving-kindness would take the place of the Temple and its sacrifices. In the centuries until the modern era, the hope of His ultimate redemption kept the Jews faithful and so gave them the determination to persist.

When Hitler killed six million Jews, the birth of the state of Israel provided a haven for the refugees and gave hope to all Jews. Many Israelis feel that Israel's defeat of the more numerous and powerful Arab states in three wars was because God acted to save them.

An interesting answer to this question was provided by a student, "God saved the Jews simply by being God." The knowledge that He was there, that His Torah is true, that the Jewish people have an on-going destiny, these buttressed the people even in the worst extremity and helped them go on to redemption.

Why did God preserve us as a people through the ages, then allow the destruction of the six million?

When someone is killed by a car, people will cry, "Why does God allow it?" An auto can carry us safely, and it can kill. A great country can protect its citizens, and it can turn into a monster and kill. The victims of the armies or of the automobiles are equally innocent. Yet we can't say that God "allows" or "prevents" either situation. Man has been given the responsibility of life, and this responsibility cannot be removed.

Judaism and the Jews have been threatened many times, but they have persisted. Half a dozen times it seemed as though the Jews and Judaism were being destroyed. The Assyrians and Babylonians threatened total annihilation. The Romans under Titus and under Hadrian threatened destruction. The Crusaders in the Middle Ages and in the 17th century the Cossack Bogdan Chmelnitzki in the Ukraine and Poland did their worst. Yet Jews and Judaism survived. Even though hundreds of thousands of Jews died for *kiddush ha-Shem,* the Sanctification of God's name, as a people and as a religion we persisted. To some Jews these tragedies were a kind of trial, to see whether they would be worthy to persist despite oppression. To most Jews, they were a kind of proof of the spiritual worth of Judaism, a religion which would not sully the world by teaching oppression, that bore the blows of the ungodly to demonstrate their own faith and dedication.

Hitler brought to his death campaign modern equipment and organization. He slew more than did any previous anti-Semite. There were also many more Jews alive. Even the worst of the mass killers of earlier ages could not slaughter six million Jews because there were not that many alive at one time.

The Innocent as Victim

In World War II, as in every war, the innocent suffered at the hands of the cruel. Millions of Russians and Poles, of Dutchmen and Greeks died because the nations of the world allowed a madman to head a powerful country. The Jews suffered the most.

We are the people who have set the standards of ethics and spirit for mankind. When evil men rebel against these standards they turn in anger on the people who gave the Bible to the world. It is not only the Jew the evil wish to slay, it is God and His laws of truth which are their major target. Judaism and the Jews have outlasted Hitler and Stalin, as they did Hadrian and many other less powerful anti-Semites. The State of Israel has been established. We can protect our own a bit better. We go forward with our people and our faith. Otherwise, we would give Hitler the victory long after his death.

Did God help us in the Six Day War?

There are people who feel that Israel's victories in the three wars she has had with the Arab states have all been miraculous. In each war Israel was seriously outnumbered, outgunned, and surrounded by enemies.

In 1948 she had no equipment and the British were helping the Jordanians. In 1967 the Russians were helping the Arabs. Only in 1956 was it Israel against Egypt on a one-to-one basis—though Egypt then had 25 million people to Israel's one and half million.

Were these three victories miraculous? By every usual standard Israel should have lost. Perhaps the victories were miraculous, but the miracles can be understood if we learn to know the spirit of the Israelis. They planned better, they trained better. They fought much harder. What carried them to their victories was their spirit. They felt that this first Jewish state in many centuries must endure. *Ein b'rera*, they said, there is no alternative.

The Miracle of Inspiration

Now, where does God come in? The inspiration the Israelis felt was so great, the bravery so compelling, that many people feel that God Himself was the inspiration. A most interesting article was written by an Orthodox rabbi that tried to prove that the victory in the Six Day War could only be a miracle. The author, Moshe Zvi Nariyah, said that God chose this generation for the miracle because the Jews of Israel truly care for their brothers, sacrifice to bring them into the land and provide for them, and are deeply concerned for the future of the Jewish people in their own land. Their reward was victory against the armies of five countries, larger, richer, better equipped.

Was it miracle or not? We do know that it was the human spirit responding bravely to the challenge of the invader.

Is Jerusalem holy to the Arabs too?

Jerusalem is a holy city to the Arabs, but it is third in importance, after Mecca and Medina. It never was a city of pilgrimage for the Muslims. Even Meshed in Persia is more important in that the pilgrim to Meshed terms himself *Meshedi*—one who has completed a pilgrimage to Meshed—as a Muslim who has gone to Mecca claims the title *hadji.*

The early Muslims built the celebrated Dome of the Rock and the great Mosque of El Aksah (the beautiful) on the Temple Mount, but never was Jerusalem a great center of Islamic studies as was Cairo or Bagdad. After the Arabs drove out the Crusaders they seemed to lose interest in Jerusalem entirely. Later the whole area was conquered by the Turks, who are also Muslims, but they treated all their subject people with equal cruelty. To the Turks Jerusalem was utterly unimportant.

Neither was Jerusalem ever the seat of an Arab government. Palestine was ruled from Egypt, Syria or Lebanon. For most of its years under the Arabs it was considered only a small and insignificant part of Syria. The local government seat was in Ramle, nearer the sea coast, and not the backwater Jerusalem had become. Under the centuries of rule of the Turks all the country was considered a minor province and was administered from Damascus.

Professor Philip Hitti of Princeton, in his great work, "The History of Syria," speaks of Syria as the greatest producer of culture in man's history. Only it turns out that almost all of that culture was born in a small province of Syria, in Palestine, and this culture came into being when the land was possessed by the Jews.

One hundred years ago there were barely 30,000 people in all of Jerusalem, more than half of them Jews, and just about all of them—Jew, Muslim, Christian—miserably poor. It was Jewish enterprise and labor that restored Jerusalem as the queen city it once was. The Arabs did not hold Jerusalem important until they realized how dear it was to the Jews.

Does Judaism believe in life after death?

Yes. Some uninformed people believe that Judaism does not. You may even see this misunderstanding appear in print, but this is wrong. It is true that the major emphasis of Judaism is on this world and our job here. Perhaps because Christianity's main thrust is concerned with life after death and Judaism's is not, people get the mistaken notion that Judaism does not believe in life after death. Judaism does not spell out what happens after death in the way that Christianity does. There are no Jewish equivalents of the editions of Dante that come with maps of Hell, Purgatory, and Paradise.

Our prayerbooks are specific, "Who revives the dead," in the *siddur;* "Who has established within us eternal life," in some modern versions. The reason traditional Jews prohibit cremation is that they believe in the physical revival of the dead, and therefore demand that the body be kept in its grave to await the resurrection.

The Mount of Olives, east of the Temple Mount in Jerusalem, has been a huge Jewish cemetery for 3000 years because tradition holds that the resurrection will take place in the Valley of Kidron at its foot—and many people wanted to be among the first to rise. One reason Orthodox Jews are buried with Israeli earth strewn in their coffins is that they believe it will mystically help transport them to the land of Israel for the rising.

The Mission of the Soul

Hasidic Jews maintain that the soul never dies and lives indefinitely. They aver that each soul has to accomplish a spiritual mission on earth, and it may occupy many bodies until it succeeds and then returns to God. This is something like the Hindu belief in reincarnation, but in Hinduism the final death is a release from the burden of life. In Hasidism, the soul is reborn until it is fulfilled.

Judaism says that as we have faith in God in life, so also do we have faith in Him in death. Life is "more than a watch in the night, than yesterday when it is past." If a soul that never existed before can be born into life, why cannot a soul which once did exist continue to live?

There are two kinds of immortality in Judaism. Immortality consists of our deeds which affect our society and our time—no matter on how large or small a scale—as well as the remembrance of these deeds, and the love and friendship we leave behind. It consists of the impress we made on people and how they were changed, for the good or for the worse, because of our lives. And these deeds and these impressions continue through the generations even long after our memory may be gone.

Judaism also teaches that the soul persists, it lives on with God. Does it have a separate existence, or is it gathered into the Godhead? This we do not really know. We will find out a moment after we ourselves die. Tradition does maintain that there is a separate, individual existence.

The *kaddish* prayer, which we say in reverence for the dead, is not a prayer for them or for their souls. It is an affirmation of life and God's power and goodness, and of our own role in the world. It is Judaism's response to death—affirmation, and faith in God.

Why praise God when someone dies?

This question arise from the *Kaddish* prayer, the prayer that is recited after death. It usually contains no mention of death. (There is a Reform version which does mention the departed, that is used in many temples.) The major portion of the prayer is praise of God and hope for the coming of His reign of peace and justice in the world.

The *Kaddish* originally was the close of the prayer service that concluded a study session. As study was considered the highest human endeavor among the Jews two thousand years ago, mourners would arrange a study session as a memorial when someone died. With the passage of time, the closing prayer with its affirmation of life came to be accepted as the prayer to be recited in memory of one who was dear to us. Gradually the custom of *yahrzeit,* the recital of the *Kaddish* on the anniversary of the death of our dear one, arose among all Jews.

The *Kaddish* praise of God is to keep us from becoming bitter in the face of death. It is to remind us of the many blessings God has given to us. It reminds us that the life that is gone was a gift from Him, as are all our lives.

It also reminds us of our places in the scheme of the world. It tells us that we are but mortals and He is God. He has all power; we have little. He is the Creator; we are the creation.

It concludes with the age-old Jewish prayer for peace, peace here on earth and on high. The word *Kaddish* is taken from the root of the word for holiness. It is a sanctification. In the face of death, we sanctify life—by affirming life and peace, both God's gifts to man.

Is there a heaven or a hell?

Liberal and Conservative Judaism do not teach that there is a hell at all. Traditional Jews believe that the soul is cleansed of sin before it returns to God. But the place of cleansing, which they call Gehenna, is not hell and no soul stays there more than a year. We absolutely say no to the very concept of hell where souls are tormented for all eternity. God would not allow any soul to be treated like that. As Leo Baeck wrote, if God did condemn any souls to eternal hellfire, He would not be God but a monster. He is God; there is no eternal Hell.

We speak of heaven or paradise, but we never say what it is. Traditional Jews speak of a place of splendor, where people will study the holy books of the Torah and the Talmud and finally understand all the wisdom that is within them—and they will enjoy the radiance of living with God.

Liberal and Conservative Jews speak only of the soul being gathered to God. He knows far better than any man what lies in store for us. We have faith in Him.

No Pitchforks, No Harps

The concept of hell as a realm of Lucifer, a fallen angel, we leave to others. It has no place in Judaism whatsoever. The idea of heaven as a place of harp playing and songs and angels too is non-Jewish. The Jewish idea of bliss is one of accomplishment.

A Hasidic *tzaddik,* Ber of Mezritch, said, "A man's kind deeds are used as seed in the Garden of Eden. Thus every man creates his own paradise."

The great Iberian statesman and Biblical commentator, Isaac Abravanel, wrote, "The reward of the souls in the world beyond is their ability to attain the true concept of God, which is the source of the most wonderful felicity" (Commentary on I Samuel 25:29).

What should we do with the body after death?

Jewish tradition says that the body returns to the elements of which it was composed. Providing a metal coffin or protecting the coffin in a vault, as some people do, is against Jewish tradition. The metal or concrete only delay the process of decomposition. The deceased benefits not at all, and moneys that might better be spent on the living are wasted underground. Any pride or pomp in a funeral is completely contrary to Jewish understanding, which stresses the equality of all in death.

The body is dear to us in life; in death it is treated with respect and laid to rest. Judaism does not hold with the custom of embalming the body and painting the face and then putting it on display for the neighbors before the funeral. This is a new custom borrowed from a different heritage and is cruel to the mourners and disrespectful to the dead.

Autopsies and Transplants

Although traditional Jews are very much against autopsies, they are not against transplants. All Jews agree that if the cornea of the eye or some other organ can be of help to a living person, it should be used. Indeed, it is a blessing.

Liberal Jews differ in allowing autopsies. Traditional Jews allow them only when it can be shown that the discoveries made in an autopsy may save the life of a person. Liberal Jews agree that physicians learn from the gradual accumulation of knowledge garnered from autopsies and that this is a major help in discovering methods for treating diseases. This is too general a statement for Orthodox rabbis, who demand that the autopsy be concerned with a particular patient and not be just a general help for the future.

Cremation

Many Reform rabbis and some Conservative rabbis will permit cremation. Cremation was considered pagan and condemned. There is no possible relationship with paganism today, which is why some rabbis permit it.

Traditional Judaism allows only a simple wooden casket made without nails, so that the passage of the body to be at one with the earth is not delayed. In Jerusalem bodies were and are buried in their shrouds, without any coffin at all.

Any display of wealth or ostentation at a funeral is false. So too impressive monuments or mausoleums are unnecessary and are alien to Jewish thinking and tradition. They are memorials to the least important aspects of life.

Death claims all men at last. All are united in the mighty brotherhood. Let us go in humility as well as in faith.

Why do we grow old and die?

There is rhythm to life, "seedtime and harvest, cold and heat, summer and winter, day and night" (Gen. 8:22). Life has beginning, middle and end.

The round of the seasons continues, and so too the round of life. Nothing endures forever, except God. Mountains grow old and slowly decay, planets and stars burn out.

God has implanted mortality in all things, in all animate beings and in man. Otherwise the world would forever be in a condition of stasis, unmoving, unchanging, never young or old. This would not be life; it would be more akin to *rigor mortis.* Even paradise in Jewish legend is a place of study and growth.

Birth presumes death. If there is beginning, there must be an end. The curve of life presupposes growth and decay, rise and fall. Without this recognition of the finiteness of man and the world, there could never be attaining, never even desire or hope. Only when man can measure his existence and is conscious of time's passage is he truly human. If he were immortal, time would have no meaning.

The Thrust into Age

Man may lengthen his years by medical research and scientific study. Even if we manage to surpass Moses' hundred and twenty, yet we remain mortal—at best postponing the inevitable. The greatest of us is consumed by time.

Man in his rationality is conscious of his mortal nature. His awareness that he is enmeshed in the web of time causes him to mark off the segments —and also to anticipate his own demise.

This consciousness of mortality profoundly affects our evaluation of life and death. We cannot live wholly existentially, caught up in the experience of the here and now of the hour. Time is passing and we cannot grasp it nor slow it down. The seconds are grains of sand that will run out of our personal hourglass, our lifeglass.

This means that we are prodded to make something of our lives before they are utterly gone. "Teach us to number our days so we may get us a heart of wisdom" (Psalms 90:12).

Death as such is not tragic. It is the close of the natural arc of life. Only when people die young or relatively young can we speak of tragedy. And yet, young or old, there is profound sense of loss, there is deep abiding sorrow.

Judaism says that our lives do not disappear. Nothing we do is entirely lost. It is reflected in future generations, for we build upon the lives of those who have gone before us. Like the coral which builds atolls of permanence in the endless ocean, we build in our lives not only for our own sake but for the sake of our children and theirs after them.

Even more, life continues in God. All is permanent—within God. "Weeping may lodge for the night, but joy comes in the morning" (Psalms 30:6).

How does Judaism differ from the teachings of Jesus?

Judaism and Christianity agree in many details in their teachings of ethics. This is not surprising as Jesus was the son of the synagogue and reflected the ethical teachings of the Torah and the rabbis of his era. The Sermon on the Mount is a great sermon, but each of the phrases has been shown to be taken from Jewish devotional literature (see Gerald Friedlander, "The Jewish Sources of the Sermon on the Mount," London, 1911).

Yet Jesus' teachings do significantly differ from rabbinic Judaism. Three times is the "Render unto Caesar" theme presented (Matt. 22; Mark 12; Luke 20). This concept seems to divide the world into a kind of dualism, with areas that are man's or belong to the government, and areas that belong to God. Judaism's reaction is that all the world is God's, and all men are God's creation, and all are to be judged by God's standards. The person who attempts to excise any aspect of life from God's rule or from being judged by God's criteria is fooling himself and denying the basic concept of the Torah. God and His standards cannot be limited.

A second area of disagreement is proposed in Jesus' remark that if a man slaps you on one cheek, you must offer him the other (Matt. 5:39; Luke 6:29). This seems unreal to us. If a person injures you without provocation, you must attempt to reason with him, to find if he believes he has provocation—and remove the cause if it exists. If there seems to be no valid reason for his violence, then it is not only fatuous, it is criminal to allow him to continue. The major idea is to induce him to stop, but his continued assault is not to be borne if we can force him to stop.

Meeting violence with undue retaliation is also wrong. But a Hitler or a Stalin when appeased merely continues his depredations and is heartened into increasing them.

How do we determine when the offered violence must be countered? This is not simple. We must learn to be discerning, to respond with all the wisdom we possess— and with compassion. But we must learn to defend ourselves when attacked.

Dare We Judge?

A third area of disagreement has to do with judging, "Judge not and you shall not be judged" (Luke 6:3; Matt. 7:1). Judaism's reaction is to quote

Scripture, "I have set before you life and death, the blessing and the curse. Therefore, choose life that you may live" (Deut. 30:19). If we refuse to choose, to judge, even at times to condemn, we become morally neuter—and this is almost as bad as being evil, for it opens the world to the proliferation of evil. Choosing means judging, for it means discriminating between men, their philosophies, their actions. We must learn to condemn that which is evil and try not to condemn the man who does the evil, so that we may turn the man to the good. This is not easy, but who ever said that moral judgments are easy? But failing to accept the responsibility to judge means to fail to live up to our responsibilities as men and women before God.

The Thought and the Deed

Another important difference between Judaism and the teachings of Jesus has to do with the thought of doing an evil act and its actual performance. Judaism says that if a person has an evil thought and resists it, it is much to his credit. Few of us are always proof against evil thoughts; resisting them is our greater duty.

Jesus however said, "Whoever looks on a woman with lust has committed adultery with her already in his heart" (Matt. 5:28). Our reaction to this is to say that if we are already guilty in just having the thought, why bother to resist performing the evil act?

Jesus further complicates this matter by adding, "If your right eye offends you, pluck it out and cast it from you, for is it not better for you that one of your organs should perish, and not your whole body be cast into hell?" (v. 29). This statement has been taken literally and has led to physical dismemberment. It has also been used to defend physical actions against those who disagreed with a church body.

There are strong differences in Jewish and Christian concepts of the afterlife, of heaven and hell. Judaism does speak of reward and punishment, but it is rarely emphasized as it is in most branches of Christianity. The concept of damnation and eternal hellfire is considered monstrous and beneath the level of God's compassion in almost all of Jewish thinking.

Wine into Blood

Impossible for Jews even to comprehend, let alone believe, is the doctrine of transsubstantiation. Jesus supposedly said to his followers, "For who eats my flesh and drinks my blood has eternal life. . . . As the living Father sent me, and I live by the Father, so he who eats me, he shall live by me" (John 6:48-59). So Christians aver that by eating a wafer and drinking wine or grapejuice, one—either literally or symbolically—eats the flesh and drinks the blood of Jesus. To us this is a remnant of pagan ways, as it was a feature of the worship of a number of the Greek Mystery religions.

Another point is that of faith achieved only by grace. Judaism says that a person may reach a level of faith by his own understanding and striving. Jesus considered faith the gift of grace, that is God's gift. It is not to be achieved by an individual. Only the person chosen by God can have faith (John 6:44).

Jesus even said that God is no longer the judge. He turned judgment over to Jesus (John 5:22).

Jesus then turned judgment from a discernment between right and wrong into a matter of faith: the person who believes in him would have everlasting life, but he who disagrees is eternally condemned (John 5:24). At best this denigrates God, and it denies our whole understanding of God and the Torah and the worth of a man's life.

The Ultimate Chutzpah

Perhaps our greatest disagreement, if scale be given, is his statement, "I and my father are one" (John 11:30). To us God is God and no man could ever presume to make this statement. There is additional *chutzpah* in Jesus' putting himself before God. To us it is blasphemy for any man to claim identity or equality with God. Those who believe in this match Tertullian's proud boast of believing that which is unbelievable (De Carne Christi 5).

Finally, we must hold that it is not true that Jesus brought more of the idea of love to religion than previously existed in Judaism. Jesus' teachings of love are quotations from the Torah. "You shall love your neighbor as yourself," is from Leviticus (19:18). "You shall love the Lord your God," is from Deuteronomy (6:5). Both of these quotations are integral parts of Judaism, and they are centuries older than the time of Jesus.

How does Judaism differ from Christianity?

The differences are so many that they fill books. This is a brief listing of some of the major points of controversy.

(1) The idea of original sin and that man is damned at his very conception is repugnant to Jews. We consider birth and life to be in full accord with God's plan for man, as God's first command was "Be fruitful and multiply"

(Gen. 1:28). Our prayerbooks read, "The soul which You, O God, gave to me came pure from You."

(2) The insistence that the flesh is evil and to be suppressed is foreign to Judaism. Judaism holds that body and soul are both God-given, and both should be sanctified to His service. Mortifying the flesh is a denial of God's gift of creation.

(3) The notion that Jesus was God in the form of man is beyond our comprehension. The very idea of a triune God—God somehow divided into three, with one part assuming flesh as a man—is to Jews an impossible mis-understanding of the oneness of God. Despite the long history of depiction of God in Christian art, Judaism avers with the *Adon Olam* that God has no figure nor form. He is eternal spirit.

(4) The theory that man can be saved only vicariously, that all men were damned by God until Jesus as God transformed into man voluntarily had himself crucified, and that only then was God willing to forgive some men—those who had faith in Jesus as God—this to Judaism is blasphemy. We hold that any blanket damnation of man is insulting to God's intelligence and to His compassionate nature. He especially would not condemn for the sins of others. As modern Jews view Adam and Eve as a part of Jewish myth and not historical figures, we cannot base any theology on their existence. To damn men because of them is ridiculous.

We hold that each man can attain to God's love by faith in Him and in the doing of deeds of living-kindness.

Paul and His Actions

(5) Paul abrogated the authority of Scripture and of tradition, and thus nullified the commandments of the Torah. Instead he substituted faith in Jesus as the redeemer and the sacraments as man's vehicle to salvation. No longer were deeds of loving-kindness essential for redemption. This is not only a denial of the word of God as expressed in the Torah, it is even a deni-al of Jesus' own words, for he specifically said that he had not come to change Jewish law one jot or one tittle (Matt. 5:17, 18).

(6) Paul said that Jesus was the messiah and was resurrected from the dead, and that he waits in heaven until the time comes for him to return to earth to judge mankind. Our answer is that the messiah as presented in the prophetic writings is to bring peace and justice and spiritual redemption to all mankind, and not just the promise of them. The promise was already explicit a half millennium before Jesus was born. He added not a whit. We deny that Jesus was the messiah because he accomplished none of the ob-jectives the messiah is supposed to attain.

(7) Paul dropped the Jewish festivals and substituted for them holidays supposedly based on the life and death of Jesus. He erased festivals which are established in the round of the year and in the history and growth of the Jewish people and the Jewish religion, and substituted a holiday, Easter, which seems to have its origin and practices in the ancient pagan celebrations of the vernal equinox, the death and resurrection of Mithras or Tammuz every springtime.

Later Christians added the holiday which is supposed to be based on the birth of Jesus, Christmas, but this is almost entirely a copying of the ancient myth of the birth of Mithras, including stable, star, magi, shepherds, gifts, etc.

(8) The Catholic Church substituted for Yom Kippur the sacrament of confession, which gives to the priests of the Church the right to grant absolution after hearing confessions.

To Judaism this is entirely presumptuous. It destroys the close union we believe each person should have with God Himself. It also reduces sin to the personal level. In Judaism, sin has always been both personal and communal, for even private sin contaminates the entire community, and we must therefore seek atonement not alone or with a priest-confessor, but with the entire community, joined in prayer before God

(9) Jews disagree strongly with the idea that only some human beings, those who have the correct faith, will find their way to God. Judaism believes that it has a direct way to God, but does not deny validity to any other religion that truly strives to seek Him. If a religion teaches that virtue and faith will lead us to God, then we feel it is a proper vehicle to earn God's love.

(10) And last, we do not believe that man has to be "saved" from Hell. Man is not lost to begin with. Only the most evil of men are to be considered "lost," and even they can achieve salvation if they turn from their evil and seek goodness. No man, no church, no ritual can promise anyone absolute absolution. But Judaism says the person who gives up his evil ways and turns to God, he shall find pardon.

We keep on reading in literature that the God of the Jews is vindictive, and the Christian God is the God of love. Is this at all true?

The God of the Jews is compounded in equal measure of justice and compassion. There are many passages in our Bible of unrelenting justice. There are fully as many brimming over with love and mercy.

"Vengeance is mine and recompense" (Deut. 32:35), sounds as though God is vindictive. But the rabbis said that God established timeless ethical laws by which man must live. If man scoffs at these commandments and acts in wickedness, he brings punishment upon himself. If wickedness goes unpunished, if the Covenant is broken without concern, then God's commandments, all ethical teachings, become worthless.

The rabbis added that this verse means that man must not take revenge himself, for this is God's privilege alone. In taking vengeance, man sins anew. Each act of vengeance gives birth to another, until violence becomes the rule of men or of nations.

The God of Justice and Mercy

God is a God of justice, yet also in Deuteronomy is the verse, "The eternal God is a dwelling place, and underneath are the everlasting arms" (33:27). This is the supreme presentation of God as the compassionate Father of all mankind.

And let us not forget our Bible's sublime definition of religion altogether, "It has been told you O man, what is good, and what the Lord your God asks of you: to do justice, to love mercy, and to walk humbly with your God (Micah 6:8). The usual depiction of the Lord in our sacred literature is that of a Father whose love encompasses all mankind, not only the people of Israel.

Fire and Brimstone

On the other hand, the God of the Christian Bible does not always appear as a kind, tender or forgiving Father. Often he is pictured as stern and implacable, as the incarnation of unquenchable wrath. His fierce anger is directed not only against those guilty of ethical infractions, but even more against unbelievers. Vivid pictures are drawn of lakes of fire and brimstone in which sinners will be subjected to everlasting torment despite their pleas for mercy (Luke 16:19-26; II Thess. 1:6-9).

We read, "It is a fearful thing to fall into the hands of God," and the promise of what will happen to those who refuse to recognize Jesus as the messiah (Heb. 10:29-31). The unbelievers, in Jesus' own words, will be cast "into a furnace of fire: there shall be wailing and gnashing of teeth" (Matt. 13:42). They will be condemned to eternal damnation (Mark 3:29).

The most atrocious of all ideas ascribed to God is this "eternal damnation." That God would condemn any of His creatures to be tortured to the end of eternity is completely foreign to the Hebrew Bible and to normative Jewish thought. There is purgatory in traditional Judaism, a region of cleansing, but no soul remains there longer than one year.

That God would willingly condemn all mankind to eternal hellfire because of Adam's sin is not Jewish at all. That He would not relent until His "only begotten son" deliberately had himself crucified, and thereafter accepted only those humans who were baptised in the faith of this "son" and remained adamant in damning all other human beings—this to Judaism is an abomination. This is a portrayal of a vindictive God with a vengeance. Jews cannot accept this unloving relationship with God, and Jews find it offensive that this picture is then foisted on the world as a depiction of the God of Judaism.

A Distorted View

Much of our accepted literature was written by Christians familiar only with the teachings of their church. If they had become familiar with the true Jewish understanding of God, they could not so carelessly foster their antithetical ideas.

The rabbis always said that the Tetragrammaton, the four-letter name of God YHVH, which we render as the Lord, the chief of all His names, is His expression of His quality of mercy. They say that He Himself considered mercy and compassion as His prime essence of being.

Our prayerbooks quote from the Psalms on almost every page, and they present to the Jew for his daily and Sabbath devotions the idea of a God who is infinite in His concern for His children: "Who forgives all your sins, who heals all your diseases, who redeems your life from destruction, who crowns you with loving-kindness and tender mercies" (Psalms 103:4).

He is a God of justice who punishes wrongdoing, but is quick to forgive those who would atone for their sins: "The Lord, the Lord God, merciful and gracious, long-suffering and abundant in goodness and truth. Keeping mercy for thousands, forgiving iniquity, transgression and sin" (Ex. 34:6,7).

The Gospel story of Jesus seems to fit the prophesies concerning the Messiah, or so Christians aver. Is this true?

Many facets of the Jesus story as presented in the Gospels seem to fit prophetic utterance of 500 or 600 years before. Many scholars are convinced that this is not just chance: not that Jesus lived these incidents and thus conformed to and confirmed the prophecies, but that those who wrote the four biographies of his life called the Gospels knew their Hebrew Bible and carefully tailored their reports to fit.

Birth in Bethlehem

An example would be the story of Jesus' being born in Bethlehem. Joseph and Mary lived in Nazareth, a three- or four-day journey from Bethlehem. Why would Joseph subject his pregnant wife to such a difficult trip? The Gospels speak of some census or tax requirement, which does not make sense from our knowledge of the time. We know of no need for a family to trek to its ancestral home, especially since Joseph was the head of the family and a resident of Nazareth. However King David was born in Bethlehem and the Gospels model Jesus' life on David's.

Slaughter of the Innocents

Why do Joseph and Mary take the infant to Egypt? It is to fulfill the line from the prophet, "from Egypt have I called my son" (Hosea 11:1). The excuse that they had to flee Herod's "slaughter of the innocents" makes no historical sense for that slaughter never took place. First, Herod died in 4 B.C.E. If you say that the Christian chroniclers got Jesus' birth year wrong, which seems strange, there is still no record of Herod's killing all the Jewish male children. Herod was a cruel man and capable of such an infamy but if he had done it we would know about it. He reigned in historic times and the record of his deeds is substantiated. And yet it is possible that Jesus was born in 4 B.C.E. and the chroniclers put the date four years later—in order to have Jesus enter on his public ministry at the age of 30, because David began his reign as king of the Jews as a man of 30.

The Virgin Birth

An addition to the Jesus story is the so-called virgin birth. The book of Matthew begins with a genealogy which links Joseph, the husband of Mary, with King David, so that Jesus will be of David's line. A later hand inserted the virgin birth, which means that Jesus was not the son of Joseph and thus not a scion of the house of David.

The very idea of God fathering a human child disturbed the rabbis exceedingly. Yet they were not as disturbed by this as much as by the pronouncement of the church that Jesus was indeed God.

The Criteria of the Messiah

The basic discrepancy between the prophecies and the Gospel have nothing to do with the miracles or Jesus' personal history. The prophets' depiction of Messianic times is clear, "Nation shall not lift sword against nation, neither shall they learn war any more" (Isaiah 2:4). Peace and justice and brotherhood will reign over the earth. Poverty, famine and oppression will disappear. The earth will be filled with the knowledge of God.

Whether we accept these few but fundamental concepts as the signs of the messiah's coming, or insist on the many more signs as predicted in the Bible and in the apocalyptic literature, "the fall of Rome, the deliverance from Gehenna, the elimination of the Evil Urge, forgiveness of sins, etc." (Pesikta Rabbati § 37), we see that Jesus' life and work fulfilled none of these. The Christian claim that Jesus appeared to prepare the world for the Second Coming seems to have borne little fruit.

The Jewish opinion of Jesus is that he was a man, a Jew, a rabbi. He taught a small group of followers some beautiful parables, but he added no dimension or depth to rabbinic teaching. He pronounced himself—or allowed others to announce—that he was the messiah. He died a cruel death on the cross, one shared by thousands of other Jews. A whole new religion was founded on his death, a religion which propounded a theology we cannot accept at all.

The concept of a king-messiah, a man who would lead the Jewish people to the reign of peace and righteousness on earth, was changed to that of God descended to earth and the need of this man-god to sacrifice himself so as to earn mankind's salvation from a Father-God who otherwise had doomed all mankind to roast in everlasting Hell. This to us is not only false, it is blasphemy.

Are there Jewish teachings of ecology?

Without knowing this word, the Torah and the Talmud dealt comprehensively with the idea of respect for the earth and all that grows on it, and indeed, for every thing upon the earth. The rabbis based their thinking on the Biblical injunction, "When you besiege a city for a long time, making war against it in order to take it, you shall not destroy its trees by wielding an axe against them. . . Are the trees in the field men that they should be besieged by you? Only the trees which you know are not food trees you may . . . cut down, that you may build siege-works . . . (Deut. 20:19, 20).

The rabbis took the words "you shall not destroy" *bal tashchit,* and extended them. If the injunction not to destroy held in wartime, why not in peacetime? If to fruit trees, why not to everything that produces life and nourishment? So they said a man may not shift the course of a stream lest trees dry up and die (Sifra Shofetim § 203).

Within a brief time the rabbis extended *bal tashchit* to all situations. "Whoever breaks vessels, or tears garments, or pulls down a building, or clogs up a fountain, or destroys food, violates the prohibition of *bal tashchit* (Kiddushin 32a).

Destruction Is Vandalism

They later used this principle to cover anything of use or value in the world. "It is forbidden to destroy or to injure anything capable of being useful to mankind" (Shulchan Aruch of the Rav, Hilchot Shemirat Guf VaNefesh § 14). Any wanton destruction was considered a violation of the teachings of the Bible (cf. Tosafot on Avoda Zara 11a; Baba Metzia 32a).

All persons were forbidden to destroy property, not only the property of others, but also one's own. For what we call property is not our own, it is really God's. So any destruction is vandalism and is condemned.

"The principle of *bal tashchit* entered deep into Jewish consciousness, so that the aversion to vandalism became an almost psychological reflex and wanton destruction was viewed by Jews with loathing" (Rabbi Robert Gordis, "Judaism and the Spoliation of Nature," Congress Bi-Weekly, April 2, 1971).

Destruction in War

The Jewish respect for nature as enunciated in the Torah and as practiced by Jews throughout most of their history is in contradistinction to the war policies of many ancient and modern peoples. The Assyrians practiced a "scorched earth" policy. Any nation that dared resist the Assyrian army was punished by having its cities razed and its people driven into exile. What is more, its farms and orchards were destroyed as a warning to the world.

The Romans in their siege of Jerusalem not only leveled the city, but to build their siege works they cut down every tree for tens of miles around. The once forested hills were completely denuded and erosion set in. For almost 1900 years the hills remained barren. The defoliation sprays used by American forces in Vietnam would fit under the Biblical ban.

Is there Jewish teaching on concern for animals?

Long before the ASPCA was founded, the Torah and the Talmud contained teachings which provide the philosophic and theological bases for our historic concern

The Torah has sympathy for animals, their emotions as well as their well-being. A man's ox and ass must rest on the Sabbath, just as he does (Ex. 20: 10). The ox must not be muzzled as it treads out the grain (Deut. 25:4).

As animals have life, they demand our concern. They may be man's property, but they may not be treated with contempt. Indeed, the Talmud says a man must feed his beasts before he himself eats (Berachot 40a).

The Torah says that it is forbidden to plow with an ox and a donkey as a mixed team (Deut. 22:10). The donkey would have to work beyond its strength to keep up with the much larger ox.

One may not slaughter a ewe and its offspring on the same day (Lev. 22:28) as it would be an affront. This is concern with the dignity of life altogether.

A person may not take the mother bird together with its eggs or fledglings from a nest (Deut. 22:6,7). The mother must be allowed to escape.

Living Creatures

Maimonides taught that the commandment was intended for the bird's good. Animals have feelings like those of human beings. It would be needlessly painful to the mother bird to add to the despair of losing her young to see it happen before her eyes—and then cap it off by slaying her as well. It also teaches man not to be arrantly cruel and disregard the emotions of any sentient beast.

Nachmanides cited another reason which rings loud to us today. While we are permitted to use animals for food, we are forbidden to destroy a species.

Tsaar Baalei Hayyim

The Talmud has an expression which is used often, *tsaar baalei hayyim*, "the pain of living creatures." Even slaughter for food was considered at best a necessary evil (see Baba Metzia 85a).

The rabbis forbade the killing of animals except for food or protection against marauding beasts (Hullin 7b). So hunting was considered a sport of the non-Jew. Any person who would slay an animal or bird for sport was looked upon with contempt. Animals and birds have life, they have emotions. To slay them for pleasure is not considered much less reprehensible than human torture.

A responsum of the noted Rabbi Ezekiel Landau of Prague (1717-1793) reads, "I cannot comprehend how a Jew would even dream of killing animals for the pleasure of hunting. When an act of killing is prompted by sport, it is downright cruelty" (Solomon Freehof, Treasury of Responsa, pp. 216-219).

One reason why a *shochet* (ritual slaughterer) must always be a God-fearing and pious person is that the rabbis were afraid that getting used to spilling animals' blood might innure a person to the horror of letting human blood as well.

Vegetarianism

Vegetarianism has not been central to Jewish teaching, though the Essenes and some other Jewish sects were vegetarians. Their refusing to eat the flesh of animals may be related to the feelings of the Orthodox who do not wear the skins of animals on Yom Kippur. They do not wear leather shoes or belts as an animal must be slain to provide the leather. They who ask mercy should not show that they themselves have been cruel to beasts. The Essenes, in anticipation of the final judgment, refused to slaughter beasts lest there be any sins on their souls for so doing.

Rabbi Zalman Aharon refused ever to eat meat. Once when he was ill his wife importuned him to eat some chicken, saying, "You are a good man; you should not die."

He answered, "I may be a good man, but the chicken, what was its sin?" (Al HaTorah, Mordecai Cohen, p. 36).

Kosher Slaughter

Most of us can comprehend the emotions of vegetarians and recognize their validity, and yet remain meat eaters. Jewish law regulated the slaughter of beasts and fowl for food so that there is as little pain inflicted as possible. The *shochet* must be informed and skilled, the knife must be exceedingly sharp and without nicks. The cutting of the carotid artery is supposed to produce instant unconsciousness.

Even the prohibition of using the blood is supposed to keep us from desiring blood and killing.

Would God allow the world to be destroyed?

Does this question mean just the earth? Or just the solar system? or does it include all of the cosmos? This answer is based on just the earth being involved in the destruction.

The Talmud tells us that the earth was not the first world God created. He created others and destroyed them—or allowed them to destroy themselves—as He was not satisfied with them. One reason the rabbis offered for their destruction was that their inhabitants had no free will. They were puppets of destiny. If there was no hate, yet there was no love; if there was no war, yet there was no real peace; if there was no evil, there was no true goodness, no sacrifice, no loyalty, no attainment. These worlds were meaningless, as they existed unchanging, never attaining, never achieving. But this is only Talmudic legend.

Perhaps there were worlds of evil. Perhaps they were inhabited by beings who destroyed far more than they built, until they destroyed their world. If man insists on living selfishly and brutally, he may well destroy this planet. He has the power to do so, with nuclear explosions, or in his insults to the ecological balance of nature. He may do so with incessant war, or by rupturing the social fabric of our civilization.

What would this mean? Impossible to answer, but God might turn his attention to some other world in some other system—or allow a new start to man or some other creature who might flee this ravaged earth. The possibility is there. It would be presumptuous of us to think that God's attention is directed only to this planet and the men upon it. Who would be so bold as to say that God has not His attention on beings on a dozen or a million other habitable planets or asteroids in far-distant galaxies?

Refuge from the Flood

Yet if we read the Bible aright, God when faced with a planet filled with violence, with a civilization bent on destroying itself, allowed its destruction —or destroyed it Himself—but kept the best of it alive in the persons of Noah and his family.

Sodom and Gomorrah too present us with society gone mad. Abraham pleaded with God, but not even a minyan of the just could be found. The few relatively good people—no one has ever claimed that Lot and his daughters were truly good—were rescued.

If man persists on poisoning our world, physically and morally, he may well write *finis* to his existence as we know it. There may be a saving remnant who will manage to go on. But it would be in a world ravaged and stripped of its resources.

The words of the Torah are clear: man is placed in the Garden of Eden "to till it and to tend it" (Gen. 2:15). God placed man on this earth to care for it. If he is unfaithful to his trust, he will discover to his sorrow what he had brought into being. If he learns that he can truly till it and tend it that both he and the world increase in worth, then he will fulfill simultaneously God's and nature's demands.

Do Jews believe in astrology?

At one time many Jews did. There are references in the Talmud which indicate this. Rabbi Samuel said, "The orbits of the heavenly bodies are as familiar to me as the streets of Nehardea" (Berachot 58b). Yet there is a Midrash, a rabbinic story, which contradicts this. In this Midrash, God tells Abraham that he is to be father of a great people. Abraham looks at the skies and replies that according to the stars he is not to have a son. God's response is basic to our understanding, "Cease your planet-gazing. Israel has no constellation" (Shabbat 156a; Gen. Rab. 44:14). It means that Judaism holds that people determine their own destinies, that they are not bound by fate which is determined by the zodiac.

Yet until recently almost all people believed in astrology, and so did many Jews. In the Middle Ages many prominent astrologers were Jews. Jewish interest in astrology led Jews to become astronomers. The expert knowledge of the stars they had gained became the basis of scientific studies. So the early age of exploration owes its very existence to the "map Jews," Jews of Spain, Portugal and Italy, who produced the astrolabe and many of the first maps and charts for navigational use.

Today Judaism frowns on horoscopes and astrology and refuses it any credence. Why the change? In former years it was felt that though each person was related to his star, the stars themselves were directed by God. If a person changed his moral situation, for better or for worse, God would then change the course of the star to keep it in proper relationship with the person's character. The star and the person reacted on each other, and a change on the person's part led to a change in the star's course just as a change in the star's course affected the person.

The Reign of Science

Copernicus, Galileo and Kepler altered all this. When they established the centrality of the sun and the vast distances to the stars, they destroyed the concept of man affecting the stars. This made clear that if the far-distant stars were considered to control man and his destiny, man would have no control over his own fate. This is impossible by Jewish standards, which stress the responsibility of man for his own actions and decisions. So the reading of horoscopes and any reliance on them are refused in Judaism.

Almost a thousand years ago Maimonides wrote, "Astrology is a disease, not a science .... Only fools and charlatans lend value to it" (Responsa II 25b).

Is there a God, and how do we know?

We firmly believe that there is a God, who is eternal and fills all the world. The world makes no sense without God. It is far too complicated and, at the same time, far too orderly for it just to have happened in even billions of years.

Think of how complicated a fine watch is. If you put metal pieces in a box and shook them for a hundred years or a thousand years, do you think that they would ever form a watch? Of course not. Yet a single flower is alive! True, but the flower's being alive is one more proof of God. How can anything be alive just by happening?

There are other reasons why we believe in God. God is an intelligence and a spirit who cares for man. So we find that the world is often intensely beautiful, sunrise, sunset, clouds, mountains, the sea, flowers, and so much more. These are not blind beauties, for man can appreciate them and even add to them.

Man can think and can plan ahead—this can only be part of a divine plan.

We are blessed with such great things as love, devotion, loyalty, the ability to sacrifice to others, the ability to create. Could these be the products of blind chance?

We believe that God has communicated with man, that our Holy Scriptures are the product of man's being inspired by God, and that God continues to work within man to help us build a better world, a world of spirit and love.

What is God like?

This is a question we'd all like to hear answered, but no answer will begin to suffice. The trouble is that we must use words and terms that were made by man to describe man—and try to use them for God, who is beyond men.

The great philosopher Maimonides said that all we can do is say what God is not. He is not a man or a thing. He has no body. He has no form, and needs neither food nor drink. Even if we say that God is kind or loving, we probably err, for we are using our understanding of what a kind man is or what a loving woman is as comparison, and this too is impossible.

What can we say? We can say that God is a spirit that moves throughout the universe. We can recognize Him by what He does. We can tell what He has done in the world, and what He is doing, His part in the creation of the cosmos, in the orderly procession of the stars in their heavenly courses, in growth and achievement, in inspiration. We find Him in the urge to create, in the will to create, in the desire to love.

The Torah and God

The Torah tells us that no man can see God and live. But the Torah also portrays in great detail the spirit that is God. We learn of the meaning of God's universe, of His plan for man. We are told that man is created in God's image. The rabbis said that this does not mean God's physical image—rather in His spiritual image. As God chooses between good and evil, so can we. As God creates things of use and beauty, so can we. As God produced a world where friendship, brotherhood, loyalty and love can be, so we must help produce such a world to be worthy of being created in His image.

Does God care about every person, or just famous people, or those who follow every law?

Amos was a herdsman, Elisha a farmer. Gideon was threshing wheat. But God spoke to them. God is near to every human being. That is why each of us must respond to God with the best in him. Few of us will become famous. Only a few will be truly creative. But each of us can respond with all of himself, and God will be there to help, to enrich our spirit and our lives.

Some children have asked, "How can God keep track of billions of people?" The answer is simple. Computers can store millions and millions of bits of information and retrieve any of them in fractions of a second. Certainly, God should have no more trouble than a computer.

And Judaism also says that you do not have to be perfect to earn God's love. David made wars. He even stole another man's wife, which was evil. But he cleaved to God. He atoned. He was punished. He continued to try to reach God, and he succeeded.

You may not be an Amos or an Elisha or a Gideon or a David. But you are just as human as they were. If you try as hard as they did to reach to God, to be worthy of His blessings, you may be answered as they were.

Why doesn't God help us when we need Him?

Does God not help us? He may be helping us all the time. Usually people call on God only when they think they need Him, when they are in trouble. But very likely He was there during the rest of their lives when things went well—and then they weren't calling on Him so loudly.

We must remember that our trouble is often caused by ourselves. Consider the situation: A teacher warns us to do our work, but some of us are lazy. When she is about to give us an exam, we cry to her, "Don't fail me. Help me, teacher!"

We know any teacher would refuse to respond to such nonsense. But some of us try to treat God just like that. We disobey His teachings, and then when we are in trouble we demand that He help us.

For example, a person smokes cigarettes and gets very ill. He prays to God for relief and is angry when God does not cure him.

This is also true when people live selfishly, create war or pollution, or allow slums or are bigoted. They have no real right to cry to God when things go wrong. Their duty is first to go out to correct what they have done or allowed to exist.

God Says You Must Choose

Our understanding of God and Judaism says that man has been given a trust: to reject evil and death; to choose the good and life. God has made the choice clear and has given us minds so we may act with intelligence. He has given man spirit which can lift him over his past mistakes. But God demands that we do the choosing, that we live according to our choices. As we may merit the reward, so equally are we responsible for stupid responses, for selfish choices.

Then does God help us or not? The answer is not easy. God helps but only when we allow Him to. No easy miracles. Slums do not disappear because children are innocent, but only when we band together to do away with them. Tragedy may strike, but we through faith find inner strength enabling us to build a good and rewarding life.

And all this can come into existence through God's help, which provides spirit and strength and ethical guidance.

What does it mean to be a Jew?

To be a Jew is a wonderful thing.

It means that you are a part of the world's oldest great religion. Our religion taught the world the idea of one God, the idea of God who cares for His children, the idea that all men are His children. What is more, it is Judaism that first taught that God cares whether man is good or bad, that He wants man to do good and not evil.

To be a Jew means to be a part of the Jewish people, a people with a great history, 4000 years old. The Temple stood in Jerusalem 3000 years ago and we worshiped God there. Priests and prophets led our forefathers.

The Jews also gave the world the idea of prayer divorced from sacrifice, of elevated, meaningful prayer. We gave the world the Bible and the great poetry and ethical and spiritual teachings of the prophets and the psalms.

To be a Jew means to be a part of an exciting role, to try to bring God's teachings to all men.

The Jewish people have given to the world some of its greatest men and women, in modern days as well as in olden times.

To be a Jew means to be related to our brothers in Israel, who are rebuilding our ancient homeland into one of the most democratic, most forward-looking countries of the world.

It means to be part of a people with a magnificent heritage, and an equally great future. We believe that as men come closer to living lives inspired by the ideals of the Torah, so they will bring the world closer to its intended fulfillment—and thus closer to God. It is our mission as Jews to help bring this fulfillment into being, by our own actions and the example we set to others. To be a Jew is an exciting challenge.

Why does the prayerbook call man "dust and ashes?"

The Bible says that when God made the first man, He took the dust of the earth, formed it and breathed a living soul into him. When man dies, his body returns to the dust from which it came.

Yet in Psalm 8 we read that God made man "little lower than divinity." The usual translation is "than the angels," but this is due to the timidity of the translators who were afraid to write the correct phrase lest it sound disrespectful. The Hebrew is most direct: man is compared to God and not just to the angels.

Man is a compound of the earthy and the divine, possessing both, possessed by both. He is sometimes closer to one than the other. He creates glorious poetry and music. He battles for noble causes. He also enjoys the fruits of the earth, the comforts of home and the fireside. He aims high; he is satisfied with little. He is good. He is evil. But even the simplest person has within him the breath of the living soul that God gave to us all.

A rabbi once said: Man should have a slip of paper in each of his two pockets. One reads, "I am little lower than divinity." The other, "I am but dust and ashes." Both are right.

Does God eat?

This question probably arose from reading about the sacrifices in the Temple in ancient days. If the *kohanim,* the priests, burned an animal on the altar fire after dedicating it to God, did it mean that God ate the sacrifice?

The pagans who lived then thought the gods did. They offered food and drink to their gods. In the Gilgamesh legend of the Babylonians, there is the story of a great flood. The gods who had not been able to eat any sacrifices for a long while, are famished. They crowd about the first sacrifice after the flood to eat and regain their strength. This is the primitive pagan point of view.

In the little book "Bel and the Dragon" of the Apocrypha, Daniel proves to the king that the gods do not eat or drink, even though food is laid out for them every night. The priests and their families feed on the food provided by the gullible king.

You ask: If God does not eat, why the sacrifice? Our ancestors thought that to pray one must bring a gift to God. The gift was to prove the worshiper's sincerity. Otherwise the prayer might be too cheap. Just to speak a few words of prayer seemed to them to be too easy. The sacrifice was of food, not only of animals and birds, but of flour or grain or fruits. In the Temple on Mount Moriah in Jerusalem, only a few sacrifices a day were burned entirely. In most of the animal sacrifices only a bit was burned. The rest of the beast was divided between the priests and the worshiper, and the meat was eaten in the Temple area.

But God did not eat nor was He even supposed to. The Hebrew word for sacrifice is *karban,* which means to "draw near." The bringing of a sacrifice as an act of worship was supposed to "draw near" the worshiper to God. When the Temple was destroyed, the rabbis said that good deeds, charity, study and prayer would "draw near" to God.

How can we believe that God is always with us?

A major difference between Judaism and Hinduism is that the Indian religion says that you can come into contact with the gods only by prolonged and difficult discipline, physical, mental and spiritual. So only a few people can ever communicate with divinity.

Judaism does say that the more learned a person is, the better will be his understanding of God and His ways. But it would never deny even to the ignorant the feeling of closeness to God. Hasidism especially makes much of the idea of even the simplest person being close to God.

There are many stories of the young person who is pure of heart and yet unable to pray because he can't read. He whistles or cries out, and when the congregation is shocked the rabbi explains that his action was of the greatest piety. But never did the rabbis recommend ignorance as a path to God. Study was the true way, but even the ignorant were not cut off.

The major barrier to feeling close to God for most people is that though they are surrounded by God, they never try to communicate with Him, to feel Him about them. Tevye, in Sholem Aleichem's stories, used to talk with God whenever he felt like it. Tevye knew He was always there. Sometimes God seemed to remain quiet. Tevye did not mind. A good friend is sometimes quiet and yet remains a good friend. Sometimes Tevye found his answer. It was as though God responded and Tevye was grateful and knew what he should do.

Tevye was a simple man, but many others, simple or wise, have felt just as he did. We too must be ready to pray to God, to talk with Him, so that we may know how we are to live. If we do not even ask, how can we possibly expect to hear an answer?

Why do young people die?

When young people die it is usually because of accidents. We all mourn when a young person is killed by an auto or in some other accident. Yet just because the person is young does not give him or her protection against accidents. God does not want people to be killed in accidents, but He does not stop them or protect them from their own or another's mistake or foolishness.

Sometimes a young person dies from disease, and this is an even greater shock to us, for we cannot blame any person or machine. Yet we know that man is doing his utmost to conquer disease, and this is according to God's will. The art of healing is blessed. Children who were born with serious defects now often are helped so they can live normal lives.

But there are a few diseases we can't as yet control, and when one of them strikes someone we all feel terrible. Even people who did not know the young person feel the loss. It is a loss to all mankind.

We must continue to try to stop accidents, to see to it that people live healthful lives. We must aid so that science may continue in its search for cures. And we must deepen our wisdom and our knowledge of religion so that we may find understanding.

Why is religion so widespread? Aren't there people without religion? And if not, why not?

A few dictatorships try to prohibit religion. Otherwise, there is religion in every land today. This was true in ancient times as it is now. People seek for religious answers to the grave questions and problems that confront them. Sometimes their answers seem to us to be primitive, like the beliefs of the aborigines of Australia. Other groups have reached high levels of religious thought, not only Jews, Muslims and Christians, but Buddhists and Parsees and others.

Religion tries to explain why man is here on earth altogether. We expect life to have meaning. If man is just an accident, life has no meaning. Everything we do or feel would be as unimportant as the movement of microbes. The most important things would be meaningless. Love and family and friendship would all be as the scrawlings on the sand left by the tide.

Without God the Master not only is death a complete cessation, but life itself has no more value than death. All life and its accomplishments would be swallowed up in nothingness. The most profound thought, the most glorious creation, the most touching emotion, the most gallant friendship, all would be waste.

But with religion, with a sense of God who created the world, who wanted to create man, who gave the world plan and purpose, all takes on meaning and value. Goodness has meaning and we recognize that evil is a denial of goodness. Prayer for strength and help has value. The Bible supplies wisdom and spirit. We are comforted in loss, find direction when troubled, are inspired to go on and build and do better. Religion is an important force in our lives, and in the lives of most of the inhabitants of our globe.

Why are there different religions?

Religions come from various sources. The religions of the Far East come mostly from India or Persia. But aside from the Far East, most of the peoples of the world worship in one of three religions, Judaism and its two daughter religions, Christianity and Islam.

Islam (the religion of the Muslims) is, like Judaism, a monotheism; it believes in one God. It has roots in Judaism but its ways are Arabic, as the language of its Bible, the Koran, is Arabic and its prayers are in Arabic. Its rites and its holidays are all Arabic in origin and form.

Christianity has many forms, Roman Catholic, Greek Orthodox, Coptic, Armenian, Marronite, and literally hundreds of Protestant sects. Its roots are in Judaism for it holds our Bible to be sacred. The major difference—and it is a huge one—is their belief that Jesus was the only son of God, that he was not only a Jew who lived in Israel 1900 years ago, but that he was actually God walking on earth.

We do not believe this to be true, for God is not a man. We do not think Jesus added to Judaism, and some of his followers took away a great deal.

It would be lovely if all men worshiped the same God the same way. But we do not think Jesus was God, and Christians refuse to give up this belief. We think the Bible is God's teachings, but the Muslims prefer their Arabic version and its teachings. We think there is only one God, but the Hindus prefer to believe in many. The Parsees have a religion of great beauty, but it has two deities. The Buddhists too have a high religion, but its ways are very strange to us. So what can we do? We must respect each other and keep faithful to our own understanding and our own heritage.

What is the difference between Judaism and Christianity?

Jews and Christians, as are all men, are sons of God. Moreover, Christianity is derived to a considerable degree from Judaism and contains the ethical teachings of our Bible. However, Judaism is the older religion, the first to teach there is only one God and that He cares for mankind.

Christians believe in our God, but they say God had a son they call Jesus Christ. Jesus was a Jew who lived in Israel almost 2000 years ago. He was put to death by the Romans for the crime of treason. He was nailed to a huge cross of wood. The Romans who were cruel, crucified many Jews for rebelling against Rome's imperial rule.

Some people believe that Jesus was the messiah and rose from the dead and promised to return to redeem those who believed in him. The messiah is a Jewish idea. He is a man who will bring peace and justice to the entire world. As peace and justice did not come, the Jews refused to believe that Jesus was the messiah.

There is an old story that illustrates this. A rabbi sat in school teaching his pupils. A man burst in and cried out, "Rabbi, the messiah has come!"

The rabbi looked out and said, "The messiah has not come."

"How do you know he hasn't come?" asked the man.

"Because the Arab is still beating his donkey."

There are still wars and oppression. Anyone who says the messiah has come fails to understand what we mean by messiah. Also, the idea that God should have a physical son is wrong to us. God is spirit and He created all mankind, not just one special son. The Christians also hold that there is another part of God called the Holy Ghost or Holy Spirit. To us, this destroys monotheism, that there is one God. Dividing God destroys His oneness, which is basic.

So today Christians worship in a church and hold Sunday as the sacred day of rest, though the Bible says that God sanctified the seventh day. They do not observe the holidays of the Bible as we do, but instead observe days linked to Jesus' life. We observe no man's birth or death as religious holidays.

If a Jew wins the Nobel prize or some other honor, should I be proud?

There are people who react to a Jew's winning a great honor or making a significant breakthrough in science or producing a magnificent creation in music or literature as though a member of their personal family had achieved it. There is a certain amount of family or national pride in all of us. Why do we enjoy our country's victories in the Olympics? Or even more strangely, our city's baseball or football team's victories, when chances are that few of the players are local men?

So it is entirely natural that we take pride in the achievements of a fellow Jew. We identify with him. Many Jews were as proud after the victory of the Six Day War of 1967 as though they had been one of the generals who directed the operation.

An additional reason for this pride is a reaction to anti-Semitism. When the anti-Semites seek to prove the Jew inferior, we can point with justifiable pride to long lists of men and women who have contributed notably to the world's advancement.

None of this reaction is bad except when it diminishes our acceptance of other people's contributions. Patriotism is natural and good; chauvinism is petty and bad. Chauvin loved only French things; anything by anyone else was refused.

We can take pride in Jewish achievements, as long as it does not blind us to the accomplishments of others.

What are angels?

Probably most people today still believe in angels. Many Jews do. But you do not have to believe in angels to be a good Jew, not at all.

In traditional Judaism angels are God's servants who do His bidding. Usually they do not have personality or even will of their own. Such stories as the Christian Lucifer legend, of an angel aspiring to God's throne, are incredible to Jews. There can be no challenge to God, especially not by angels, which are creatures of His will.

The Zohar, the Jewish mystical work of the Middle Ages, is filled with angelology. It speaks of various classes of angels, the *cherubim, seraphim,* and others. In the western world cherubs and seraphs are conceived of as chubby child angels or female angels, but the original concept holds them to be huge, powerful and sexless. They look more like a bull or lion with a human face than a pretty girl or fat baby, though the Talmud does say that a cherub's face is like a baby's (Sukkah 5b).

In the Bible angels fulfill God's commands and return to Him. The rabbis pointed out that three angels appear to Abraham. As each performs his mission, he leaves.

Sabbath Angels

The Talmud tells of the two angels, one good, one bad, who visit every home on Sabbath eve. They peer in, and if the table is set, the candles lit and the spirit of love and Sabbath peace prevails, the good angel says, "May it be this way next Shabbat!" The evil angel must respond, "Amen." If there is no preparation for the Sabbath and there is friction and dismay, the bad angel says, "May it be this way next Shabbat!" The good angel sighs and says "Amen." We still sing of the Sabbath angels in the song *Shalom Aleichem.*

The rabbis said that each person has two angels which accompany him, one good, one bad, who act as the urge to do good or to do evil. Most of us put little stock in angels, God needs no helpers or hinderers beyond man.

If God is perfect, why is the world in so much trouble?

The world is not God, neither is God the world. Each has an independent existence, though they are closely linked. God is in all men, but He is not man and man is not God. Each person has his own will, mind and way. Man and his society combine to achieve their destiny. Man's personal destiny is not decreed in advance. To some degree he can help influence the course of his life. But he is very much related to his own society. A child caught in the slums of Harlem, a man trying to support a family in Bombay, a woman with a dozen children and faced by more in southern Italy, these people are helpless to affect their destinies to any significant degree.

People are products of their parents' genes, parental teachings and example, the influence of their friends and society. They develop and grow and may show the inspiration of religion or not. God's teachings are clear on how to achieve a better world. The blame rests on those who do not heed these teachings.

Some religious people persist in emphasizing the less important aspects of religion, the ritual and ceremonial—or, even worse, those facets which restrict or divide, rather than those which help and bring us together. But this is not God's fault. There are some who reject religion and the religious spirit altogether, and they have produced Hitler's Nazi Germany, Stalin's Soviet Union, and Mao-tse-tung's China.

There are many people who do work for a better world, in this country, in Israel, in many lands. There has been some progress over the conditions of past ages. Slavery is gone, much disease is conquered. There is less official discrimination and perhaps a little less prejudice. We have become aware of the problems of polluted air and water and atmosphere. But of course this is scarcely the beginning. While there are slums, pollution, bigotry and war, we all have a long way to go.

The Kingdom of God

Judaism says the world is perfectable, not that it is perfect. Judaism says mankind is charged with the duty to work for this perfection, as a sacred task, as the only sensible task. The traditional prayerbook reads that this charge is *l'takken malchut Shaddai,* to prepare God's kingdom here on earth. Judaism has always understood this in an ethical and spiritual sense, to cleanse the world of evil, poverty, bigotry and oppression.

What was true in Amos' time, is equally true today. The charge is laid before each generation, and until this challenge is understood and accepted there is no other solution to the trouble of the world. God challenges: we must respond.

ANSWERS FOR THE YOUNG

How can God be everywhere at the same time?

Spirit does not occupy space. Spirit cannot be divided, nor can it be stopped. Spirit is more even than the rays of the sun, which seem to be everywhere at once, for the rays can be stopped by the leaves of a tree or by a roof or a mountain. Spirit is more even than radio waves, though we know that they go all the way to the moon and to Mars, for our scientists have worked rocketships by radio fully that far.

God's spirit is everywhere at every time. Just because there are more people in the world today to share God's spirit does not diminish Him. Just because we put astronauts on the moon does not diminish God at all. It just proves that wherever we go, God's spirit accompanies us.

The prophet Jonah tried to run away from God by taking a ship to the far distant port of Tarshish. He failed, as has everyone who tried to flee God. God's spirit fills the entire universe.

How can people feel or hear God and not see Him?

There are many things we feel or hear but cannot see—the wind, the air. We may smell something and not see it. We surely hear many things we cannot see—the thunder.

Even more pertinent to our question, we all listen to the radio or watch television, which come to us on invisible waves through the air.

Even more important than this, ideas cannot be seen or felt or heard or smelled or touched, and yet they move us. Love is invisible, and yet we hold it the most important factor in our lives.

God is invisible, and yet He moves us so that we can see Him working in our own lives.

How can God talk to people?

God talks to people in many ways. In primitive times people thought that God's voice thundered from the sky in a sort of public address system.

In the days of the prophets men understood that His voice speaks within a person. It sounds within him though it can't be heard by anyone else.

Often God seems to be heard as words or ideas leap into a person's mind —so that even though he hears nothing, his mind is filled with a message he believes to come from God . . . and because of its importance and beauty, others recognized the message as divine. Not in whirlwinds or in storms did the prophets hear from God, but in the thin small voice within them.

Another way God speaks to us is in His examples to mankind, as when history fulfills His teachings. A wicked person, a Hitler or Stalin, causes only pain or death—as the Bible tells us will happen. A good person, a great physician or scientist, a thinker or poet, brings joy and advancement to the people of the world. This too we believe is a way in which God communicates with people.

Why doesn't God speak to people today?

Our prayerbooks say that God speaks to all generations, including our own of today.

At first God spoke to the patriarchs, then to Moses. Later, He spoke with the prophets. But Judaism says that He continued to speak to the people of Israel through the great sages of the Talmud. To the Orthodox, the Talmud is just as holy as is the Bible because God's voice is clearly heard in it. The rabbis through their wisdom and dedication reached to the level of the prophets.

Since those days we believe that God speaks to man through the great and wise men of every generation. He speaks not only to Jews, but to worthy men of many nations and religions. It is our job to fill ourselves with wisdom and make ourselves holy by good deeds and so capable of hearing God.

Amos had no education, not nearly as much as you. He was a shepherd and a tender of sycamore trees. God spoke through him because of his dedication. He might well speak through you, if you have equal dedication.

What does God look like? Why is He invisible?

God does not look like a person, old or young. He is spirit, and spirit is invisible. An idea is invisible, love is invisible, even a pain is invisible, and yet they are most real. You have had a pain in your stomach and you may have cried, and when your mother asked why, you told her. She believed you. She did not ask you to take out the pain and show it to her.

You love your mother. You tell her. She doesn't ask you to take out the love and show it. The love is there and it is real.

God is invisible. He fills the entire world and there is room for everything else. It is something like music filling a room, sunlight filling the same room, happiness filling the room. We are in the room with the music, the sunshine, and we are filled with happiness, and yet these things do not fill it more than it was, though each adds a great deal—and each is invisible.

God is more than music, than sunshine, than happiness. He is the place of the world. He was there before the world was. His is the energy, His is the matter, His is the space. He is the world and far, far more.

How old is God? Why does He never die?

God is neither young nor old. He was not born nor was He created. He existed before time was born. He cannot die. God does not exist in time, though everyone and everything else does. Time exists in God, so He is not affected by it. Even planets and stars, like mountains, grow old. God does not. Scientists tell us that matter and energy are different forms of the same thing, ever changing. Long after billions of years have passed and the sun has gone, God will be. He will be neither older nor younger than He is now. He is.

How does God "listen" to us?

God does not "listen" to us with "ears." Talking to Him is not the only way we communicate with Him. If we live good lives, if we try to live up to the teachings of the Torah, God sees that we are worthy of His blessings. If we only pray with words that are not really part of our lives, He knows that our prayers are not in earnest.

If we have tried to be good, have tried to understand the message of the Torah and what God wants us to do with our lives, then our prayers are part of this trying to do well—and He understands and responds.

Another important thing to remember is that God seems capable of saying no to us when we deserve it. If we pray for something stupid or trivial, or for something we do not deserve, He may well refuse to listen. When does He listen? When our prayers are part of our lives, a natural part of living according to His ways.

Will I ever see God?

Please remember, we never see God with our eyes, for God is spirit, not a physical thing that eyes can see.

In the Torah we read that Moses asked to see God's face, and even he who spoke with God regularly, was denied (Ex. 33:20). But God said, "I will cause all My goodness to appear before you."

So we can say that we see God in the way He works in the world, in people who are divinely inspired to do great acts, in the beauties and wonders of nature. We believe we see God at holy hours in our lives, when a child is born, at the moment of death, in the holiness that we at times reach in prayer together.

Did God create man, or did man create God?

Some people feel very smart asking this question. What they really mean is this: Ancient man could not answer these hard questions: Who created the world? Who created man? Who gave the world direction? Why is there order? A kernel of wheat produces wheat, not barley; there is natural law. To answer these questions the Hebrews created the idea of God, the being who created and directs all. So, these people say, man created God as much as God created man.

The response is simple. Abraham discovered God; he did not create Him. God existed long before Abraham began to search. The world had growth and order, though it was not fully realized by man, long before Abraham was born. The prophets and other great thinkers have been intent on discovering His way, but not one of them thought that he created God.

How do we know there is only one God?

The *Sh'ma,* which is the basic watchword of Judaism, says that God is one. If God is everywhere, if God is truly God, there can be only one. Otherwise He must share His power, His function, His being with whatever other "God" you might try to imagine. Any second deity reduces God, so that He is not the sole creator and guide of the universe. That is why Judaism disagrees fundamentally with Christianity or any other religion that attempts in any way to divide God. God cannot be divided.

Our Jewish understanding that there can be only one God means that the world is a unitary whole. The entire cosmos as well as a single amoeba is created by the one God. All life comes from Him and only from Him.

Men may understand Him differently, but the Allah of the Muslims, the Atman of the Hindus, and the Great Spirit of the Amerinds are all related. Each is an expression of the one God.

Is God alive?

We can't use words that describe men or animals for God. God can't be compared to men or to animals.

It is like saying that God is large, immense, huge. He fills the universe. Any word we would use is not enough. When we think of big we think of an elephant or a whale—or we think of a mountain. But even if we tried to compare God to the whole earth, or the sun, or the solar system, we are not beginning to think big enough. God fills the universe, and yet He is far greater than all the universe.

So to use the word "alive" concerning God is very different from saying a person is alive or a lion is alive. God is. He exists. The *Adon Olam* says He was, He is, He will be. Before time began, God was. Long after time is done, God will be. He is the life of the world. We live in Him. Yes, God is alive.

What is important about God?

The rabbis said that God is "the ground of the universe." This means that the whole universe is in God. Nothing exists except according to God. Without God the world would not exist, and most certainly you would not exist either.

God has set the way we must live in the teachings of the Torah. When we do not think His teachings are important, we bring trouble, failure, war and unhappiness to ourselves and to those about us.

We must all learn what God's will is, for it is most important. God wants the world to get better. He wants you to lead a good life. We think He wants us to be Jews because our religion will bring us close to His teachings of goodness, of brotherhood, of spirit. These are the most important teachings of the world, and they come from God and His Torah.

How did God make people?

The Bible tells us that God created Adam and Eve out of the dust of the earth by breathing into them a living soul. This beautiful story explains the way our ancestors understood the beginning of mankind, but it is not a scientific or factual presentation.

We Jews today agree with science that the world evolved—that is, slowly grew—from simple forms of life to the more advanced, from one-celled creatures to fish and mammals and finally to man. So too the Genesis story shows God creating the world one stage at a time, ending with man and woman. We can say that it is a poetic form of the way the world did evolve or grow.

Even more important, we learn great religious truths from the Genesis story, that all men are descended from the first man, so that no one can say he is better; so that just as the world was started with only one man, each person is of infinite value to God. And we learn that God is the creator and the father of all.

Might astronauts discover a higher form of life than man on another planet?

Man may be the highest form of life on earth, but there is no reason why some other planet might not have a higher form. If so, would this prove anything concerning God?

We think that God is the God of all the universe. Finding higher forms of life would go to prove that God's presence is everywhere.

If higher forms were found and they had a religion based on the idea of one God who cares that His creatures do good deeds out of love for Him and their fellows, it would be a religion very close to Judaism. This religion would not use Hebrew or observe our holidays, but the basic ideas would be precisely the same as ours. It would agree with all of Judaism's most important teachings.

How does God help people?

God helps in many ways. He has given man spirit to do wonderful and beautiful deeds. He has given people minds to seek and to discover ways of help and healing. He has placed within man loyalty and brotherhood, to make us worthy of His blessings. He has shown us how family love can bring great and lasting joy. He has given us a magnificent world in which to live, and has given us the desire to develop it, to make it even more wonderful.

He has given us the Torah and the teachings of the prophets and sages, so that we may understand what our goal in life is, and find through our understanding the ways of goodness.

And when people are in trouble, they pray to God and with His help find strength and courage to go on and frequently to overcome trouble.

If God is good, why do evil things happen?

The most important thing is that God is good. He allows man to be good or bad, as man himself wants to be. If you want to be good, God will help you; if you want to be bad, He will allow it.

The world was not made perfect. Man's chief job is to help make the world better. Man is God's partner in making things better. People who bring health and healing, who discover new ways to feed the hungry or to house the homeless, to educate the ignorant, to bring beauty and knowledge —they are doing God's work as His partners.

Evil is real. There are people who live in slums, who go hungry, who can't get a good education, who can't get a job because of prejudice or because they were never given a chance to learn how to work. But God did not do these things—man did. God wants you and me to work to overcome them. There is evil, but it is your duty to help rid the world of it.